Stained Glass Mosaics

Projects & Patterns

George W. Shannon, Pat Torlen & Greta Torlen

Sterling Publishing Co., Inc. New York

A STERLING/TAMOS BOOK

A Sterling/Tamos Book

First paperback edition published in 1999 by
Sterling Publishing Company, Inc.
387 Park Avenue South, New York, N.Y. 10016

TAMOS Books Inc.
300 Wales Avenue, Winnipeg, MB, Canada R2M 2S9

10   9   8   7   6   5

© 1998 by George W. Shannon, P. Torlent, G. Torlen

Distributed in Canada by Sterling Publishing
℅ Canadian Manda Group, One Atlantic Avenue,
Suite 105
Toronto, Ontario, Canada M6K 3E7
Distributed in Great Britain & Europe by Chris Lloyd
at Orca Book Services, Stanley House, Fleets Lane,
Poole BH15 3AJ England
Distributed in Australia by Capricorn Link (Australia)
Pty Ltd.
P.O. Box 704, Windsor, NSW 2756 Australia

Design Arlene Osen
Photography Jerry Grajewski, Custom Images

Printed in China
All rights reserved

Canadian Cataloging-in-Publication Data
Shannon, George (George Wylie), 1961–
        Stained glass mosaics : projects & patterns
        Includes index.
        "A Sterling/Tamos book."
        ISBN 1-895569-33-8
1. Glass craft.   2. Mosaics.   I. Torlen, Pat, 1960–
II. Torlen, Greta.   III. Title.
TT298.S54 1998   748.5'028'5   C98–920039–6

Library of Congress Cataloging-in Publication Data
Shannon, George, 1961–
        Stained glass mosaics : projects & patterns / George W.
    Shannon, Pat Torlen & Greta Torlen.
            p.   cm.
        "A Sterling/Tamos book."
        Includes index.
        ISBN 1-895569-33-8
        1. Glass craft—Patterns. 2. Mosaics. 3. Glass painting
    and staining—Patterns. I. Torlen, Pat, 1960– . II. Torlen,
    Greta. III. Title.
    TT298.S42   1998
    748.5'028'5—dc21   98-12236
                                                   CIP

Sterling ISBN 1-895569-33-8 Trade
            1-895569-54-0 Paper

For Hanna Torlen
With special thanks to
Betty Shannon
Lynn Sinclair
Brianna Stark

Thanks to The Assiniboine Park Conservatory, English Gardens,
and Leo Mol Sculpture Gardens staff in assisting with
photography locations.

The advice and directions given in this book have
been carefully checked, prior to printing, by the
Author as well as the Publisher. Nevertheless, no
guarantee can be given as to project outcome due to
the possible differences in materials and the Author
and Publisher will not be responsible for the results.

Contents

Introduction   5
Stained Glass Mosaic Construction   6
Basic Techniques   13
Stained Glass Mosaic Decorative Projects   25
Construction Techniques   26
  Direct Method   26
  Indirect (Reverse) Method   29
    Making wood base/support structures   32
    Mounting wall hangings and mirrors   34
Flowers & Herbs planter boxes   35
Snakes & Lizards cactus pots   38
Old Tiles terra-cotta pot   41
Lily Pond birdbath   43
Lotus & Dragonfly wall hanging   47
Cock-a-Doodle-Dude trivet   50
Sunflower wall hanging   52
Relativity wall hanging and trivet   54
Distraction wall hanging and trivet   57
Stained Glass Mosaic tabletop   60
Fish Faerie backsplash   62
In-the-Eye-of-the-Beholder wall mirror   65
Stained Glass Mosaic Garden Stones   69
Construction Techniques   70
  Make your own garden stone form   76
Garden Stones tabletop and chairs   79
Iris Duet   80
Flower Power   80
Mr. Sunshine   82
Ying & Yang   84
Eternity   85
Grapes   86
Sunflower & Ladybug   88
Snake & Lizard   90
Sun-sational   92
Interlocking Footprints   93
About the authors   95
Index   95

The art of mosaic as we know it today involves adhering many small pieces of glass, marble, stones, or other found objects to a surface to create an elaborate and detailed decorative design.

The first examples of primitive mosaic technique using pebbles and mortar were found in floors of houses uncovered near Ankara, Turkey, dated to the 8th century BC. This method was refined over the next few hundred years, but by the end of the 4th century BC, the natural pebble technique was abandoned in favor of marble or limestone pieces cut to uniform size and shape, called *tesserae*. As the technique progressed, Hellenistic Greeks and Romans were able to achieve fine detail with a greater variance of tones, yet the mosaics lacked brilliance because of the stone medium.

Between the 3rd and 1st centuries BC glass tesserae of smalto or colored opaque glass in pure tones of red, blue, and green were introduced. They were cut from large slabs of glass and were used mostly for wall and vault mosaics. Elaborate decoration of fountains, altars, and wall murals was now possible. The use of gold and silver smalti, made by sandwiching thin layers of the precious metals between the glass layers before cutting them into tesserae, added another dimension to the art. The extensive variety of colors and the reflective qualities of the glass and gold gave Early Christian architecture a rich appearance. The use of mother-of-pearl, semi-precious stones, and other materials created even more sumptuous effects.

The grand style of mosaics reached its zenith during the Byzantine era (4th to 14th century). This style, known as the "classical system," integrated architecture and decoration and was associated with the imperial court of Constantinople. Walls were now completely covered and the figures in the pictures were larger and more prominent to give more definition to the religious message being portrayed. The tilting of tesserae pieces to reflect the light added a whole new perspective to the art form. Setting tesserae in wavy lines to model faces and using silver cubes to add more sparkle added a realism previously not achieved. Greek craftsmen were famed for the technical subtleties needed to execute mosaics of such high standards and these artisans were summoned from Byzantium to do their work in other great cities.

During the Italian Renaissance there was a gradual decline in mosaic art. It was not revived until the 18th century when a studio was set up in the Vatican to produce works for St. Peter's Basilica.

During the 1890s and early 1900s the Art Nouveau period had a great impact on the decorative arts and architecture. Antoni Gaudi brought many new ideas to the art of mosaic by using colorful tiles and fragments of found objects to cover the sinuous lines of the exteriors of public buildings in Barcelona, Spain. Famed artists Gustav Klimt and Marc Chagall had their paintings interpreted into mosaic pieces during this period. Another major change to mosaics at this time saw commercially mass-produced tiles used as an inexpensive form of decorative covering for exterior walls, patios, and swimming pools.

In the latter half of this century interest has been renewed as traditional mosaic art has been revived in Italy and other parts of the world using the Byzantine method. New and innovative techniques are also being developed and practiced by artists and hobbyists.

In recent years, stained glass enthusiasts have embraced the methods of mosaic fabrication. Marrying traditional mosaic construction techniques with stained glass materials and equipment, a modern method of this fascinating art form has emerged. The wide range of colors and textures of stained glass, combined with the ease with which it can be cut, makes intricate shapes as well as traditional tesserae possible for some extraordinary effects.

Most of the tools and materials required to construct a mosaic project are already being used by anyone working in stained glass. Because of the popularity of this craft, equipment and supplies are readily available at stained glass supply shops and hardware stores. Most glass supply shops are familiar with mosaic construction and can assist the beginner in selecting the appropriate tools and glass.

Surfaces as diverse as concrete birdbaths and wood planters can be covered with mosaic to turn a household accent into a work of art. Garden stones can create a fanciful walkway and add to the beauty of a natural setting. The patterns found in this book can be adapted to suit any type of project and may serve as inspiration for your own future designs.

Stained Glass Mosaic Construction

Various materials and tools, commonly found around the home and at local hardware stores or home and garden centers, can be used to construct the glass mosaic projects in this book. As well, you'll need a few tools and supplies specifically designed for stained glass and mosaic fabrication. Most urban centers have at least one retail outlet that caters to stained glass craftsmen and several companies offer a mail order service. Check your telephone directory yellow pages for these listings. If you know someone who has worked with stained glass or done mosaic fabrication, ask them for recommendations. A wide selection of tools and materials is available. Finding the tool that best suits your needs or the right type of grout or cement to complete any project in this book will not be difficult.

Materials

Glass   In place of the traditional tesserae, stained glass or art glass is used to construct the mosaic projects in this book. Once you have mastered a few simple cutting techniques, you will find that art glass is easy to cut, comes in an endless variety of color combinations, and is readily available at your local stained glass supply shop. We recommend the use of colorful and contrasting opaque glasses for the best effect. Choose glasses for their reflective surface qualities rather than their light transmitting properties, which are favored for traditional stained glass work. Adhesives and cement can be seen behind translucent glass, and they often detract from the glass color. This is not the case with opaque glasses. One notable exception is iridescent cathedral glass, and it is used in several projects in this book.

Glass nuggets and jewels   These pieces of glass come in a selection of colors, sizes, and shapes and can be used to accent any mosaic piece.

Ceramic tiles and china   Consider using interesting ceramic tiles or pieces of household china and crockery in areas of your mosaics. There are many exciting patterns and textures available that you can add to give your mosaic a distinctive overall design.

Adhesive   There are several types of adhesive available for bonding the many glass pieces of a mosaic to the surface of a project. The adhesive must be suitable for your project, so read labels carefully. The base material (what you are bonding the glass to), the location, and the purpose of your finished mosaic must be taken into consideration when choosing the adhesive. Use a nontoxic variety whenever possible.

Grout   Grout is used to fill the spaces, known as interstices, between individual pieces of glass. In addition to giving the project a finished look, grout adds strength, covers sharp edges on the glass, and helps to level the surface of the mosaic. Grout comes in many colors or can be tinted to create desired shades. The grout you choose should suit the location of the project and its intended use.

Premixed mortar cement   This cement was used to produce the mosaic garden stone projects in this book. Premixed portland cement and sand, with the addition of water, is all you need to produce a fine grade mortar cement to give your mosaic garden stones a smooth, even finish. This cement is found at hardware stores and home and garden centers.

Tints   Tints can be added to grout and cement to achieve a desired special color. They are made specifically for these products and are available at commercial cement plants, hardware stores, and some stained glass shops.

Petroleum jelly   A thin layer of petroleum jelly rubbed onto the sides and bottom of the mold of a mosaic garden stone will ease its removal from the mold.

Clear adhesive-backed vinyl   For the indirect method of mosaic construction, a sheet of clear adhesive-backed vinyl is required to hold the individual pieces of glass in place, to prevent movement of the pieces while working on the project, and when pouring the cement. After laying the mosaic pattern down on the work surface, the adhesive-backed vinyl (sandblast resist or contact paper) is cut to the overall size and shape of the mosaic. The paper backing is removed and the vinyl is placed over the pattern with the adhesive back facing upward. The pattern can still be seen as the glass pieces are laid onto the adhesive backing in the appropriate position.

Reinforcement wire   To add strength and durability to mosaic garden stones, a reinforcement wire is added when the cement is poured. Galvanized hardware cloth, either ½ in (1.3 cm) or 1 in (2.5 cm) mesh size, can be purchased at your local hardware store.

Plywood and wood moldings Plywood (½ in to ¾ in or 1.3 cm to 1.9 cm) and various wood moldings and trims may be required to construct molds or frames to complete some of the projects. Instructions and/or alternatives are given where necessary.

Bases or support structures Glass mosaics can be built on many different bases or support structures. Ready-made wooden planters, concrete birdbaths, terra-cotta pots, and plywood frames are just a few examples. Suggestions and ideas for bases are given with each project and instructions are supplied for bases that you can make yourself.

Equipment

Permanent waterproof fine-tipped marker   This tool is used to outline the pattern pieces on the glass for accurate cutting. For dark and opaque glasses, a silver or gold marker works well.

Drawing equipment (small square, pencil, eraser, cork-backed ruler or straightedge, grid paper, tracing paper, carbon paper, marking pen, compass, scissors, light card stock) These drawing materials and tools are used to make pattern copies, draw and score straight lines, verify

angles and alignment, and make templates.

Traditional glass cutters A traditional glass cutter is required for the accurate scoring and breaking of individual glass pieces to fit the project pattern. Two common types are dry wheel and oil-fed. An inexpensive steel wheel cutter has a larger steel cutting wheel and is usually disposed of after each project. A lubricant must be applied to the steel wheel before each score is made. This is a good choice for beginning stained glass or glass mosaic fabrication crafters. For those doing more than one project, a self-lubricating cutter with a smaller cutting wheel made of carbide steel and a reservoir for oil, is more expensive but will last for many years. Also its smaller size wheel cuts more accurately. Popular models have either a traditional pencil-shaped barrel or a pistol grip handle. The pistol grip handle helps people with limited strength in their hands and reduces fatigue.

Glass mosaic cutters or nippers Specially designed glass mosaic cutters are used to cut or nip shapes out of smaller pieces of glass. The plier-shaped cutter has two long-lasting and replaceable carbide wheel jaws and is used like scissors. Tile nippers found at the local hardware store may also be used but may not last as long or cut as accurately.

Breaking/grozing pliers Breaking pliers have flat smooth jaws to grip and break off scored pieces of glass. Grozing pliers have narrow, flat, serrated jaws to nibble away unwanted bits of glass to make the piece fit the pattern. Combination pliers combine the uses of breaking and grozing pliers. The top jaw is flat and the bottom jaw is concave: both

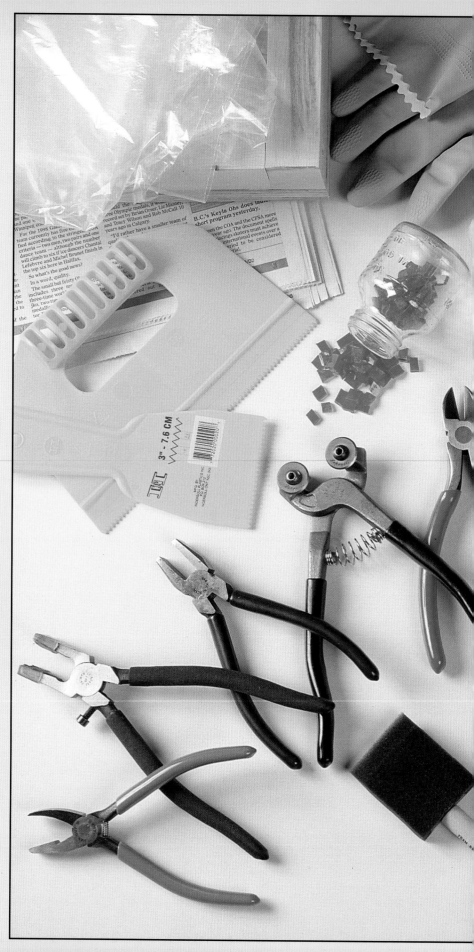

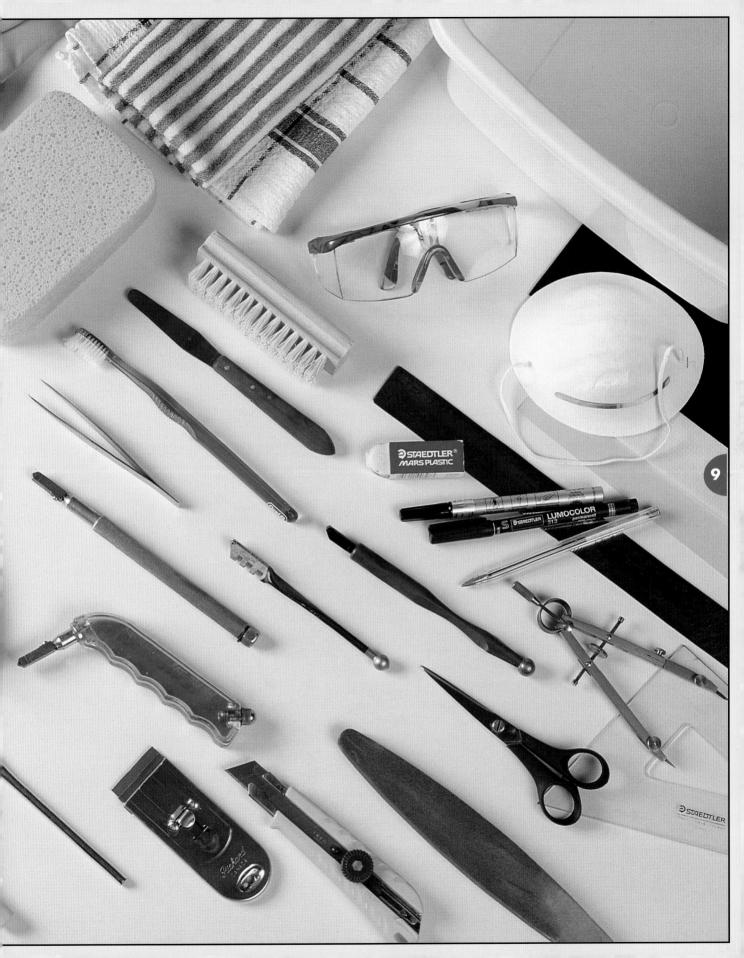

are serrated. These are the most popular pliers for hobbyists.

Running pliers   Running pliers are designed to apply equal pressure on both sides of a long and straight or gently curved score line forcing the score to "run" or break along its length. With practice, they can be used to start breaks on more difficult score lines. Running pliers are manufactured from metal or plastic. Metal running pliers have a concave jaw (placed on the top side of glass) and a convex jaw (placed on the underside of glass) that allows the breaking of narrow pieces of glass. They also have the strength to carry a "run" over a longer distance. Plastic running pliers have 3 teeth (2 on the top jaw and one on the lower jaw). These pliers are limited in how narrow a piece they can break, since all 3 teeth need to be in contact with the glass, and they have plastic handles which flex and tend to reduce the length of the "run." Some pliers have a central guide mark on the top jaw to assist in aligning the pliers on top of the glass correctly. If yours do not, simply draw on a guide mark with a permanent waterproof marking pen.

Carborundum stone   This is a small rectangular block made of hard carbon compound and silicon, and is used to file sharp edges off pieces of glass. The stone must be kept wet when smoothing the rough edges of the glass to help keep minute glass particles from becoming airborne.

Glass grinder   Complex and detailed shapes, and more sophisticated and creative designs using stained glass are now possible with the aid of a glass grinder with diamond coated bits. Rough and uneven edges of cut pieces of glass can be smoothed and ground to fit a pattern more accurately. Excess glass on tight inside curves can be ground away, reducing the risk of cracking during the breaking or grozing process. A reservoir containing water traps the dust produced when grinding and helps prevent hazardous airborne glass particles. A face shield and backsplash are recommended to contain any larger glass chips or overspray of water that may occur during the grinding process. NOTE A glass grinder is not necessary to complete the glass mosaic projects in this book although those craftsmen with access to a grinder may wish to use it. A carborundum stone may be used in most instances if some glass pieces require smoothing or don't fit, or a slight design change can simplify the cutting of a pattern piece.

Small containers or jars   In the preparation of mosaic projects, many small pieces of glass need to be cut. Small containers or jars help keep the glass pieces sorted by color and size.

Molds and forms   Many commercial molds and forms can be purchased for the construction of glass mosaics. Some of the project patterns in this book will fit into these molds but we have also given instructions for making your own. You can also use inexpensive plastic food storage containers and springform baking pans as your forms. Secondhand shops and garage sales are a great place to hunt for things that can be put to use as a form or mold. (Any item used for a mold or form should not be used again for the storage or preparation of food.)

Mixing containers and manual mixers   Containers are required to mix cement. Their size will depend upon the amount of cement to be mixed. A number of inexpensive manual cement mixers are available for making small batches of cement and save time and energy if you plan to make a number of mosaic garden stones.

Tweezers   This instrument helps to position small pieces of glass on patterns and clear adhesive-backed vinyl.

Wire cutters   This tool, also known as snips or sidecutters, is used to cut the reinforcement wire for mosaic garden stones.

Notched trowel   This tool is used to apply and evenly spread adhesive on the base material that will hold the glass mosaic pieces. Trowels come in many sizes and shapes so choose one that suits your project.

Sponges   A damp sponge is needed to wipe excess grout off glass surfaces before the grout is allowed to dry.

Brushes   Small craft brushes can be used to apply adhesive in small or hard-to-get-at areas. In the final cleaning and polishing stages, a variety of brushes helps to remove excess dried grout.

Utility knife   A utility knife has a variety of uses including trimming the clear adhesive-backed vinyl, cutting out paper pattern pieces, and clearing away excess adhesive and grout.

Razor blades/paint scrapers   Use these to scrape away unwanted adhesive, grout, and cement from the surface of any glass mosaic project.

Polishing cloths   Clean, dry cloths are used to buff the finished surface of mosaic pieces. Natural fibers such as cotton are best.

Newspaper   Rubbing the surface of a finished mosaic garden stone with newspaper lifts and removes debris while polishing at the same time.

Newspaper is not recommended for cleaning light colored grouts.

Woodworking tools Most projects in this book can be made with prefabricated molds or bases. If you wish to make your own, a variety of woodworking tools may be required. A list of required tools, materials, and instructions for the construction of forms and bases upon which to build your mosaic is listed where applicable.

Dust mask or respirator Wear protective breathing apparatus when handling or mixing cement and grout powders.

Safety glasses or goggles Wear protective eye gear when cutting glass.

The work area

Choose a comfortable working space with enough room to spread out the project. A working area requires:
• A large, sturdy table or workbench with a smooth, level work surface (preferably plywood), at comfortable working height (around waist level).
• Good overhead lighting (natural light if possible).
• An electrical outlet with grounded circuit for glass grinder.
• An easy-to-clean hard-surface floor.
• A rack or wooden bin with dividers to store sheets of glass in an upright position to prevent glass surface scratches. Use a cardboard box for smaller pieces.
• A window fan for good ventilation when working with adhesives, grouts, and cements.
• A supply of newspaper to cover work surface for easy cleaning.
• A bench brush and dust pan to clear work surface of glass chips and other debris.
• Access to water for mixing grouts

and cements, using glass grinder or carborundum stone, and cleaning projects.
• A light table for tracing patterns onto hard-to-see-through glass (glass mosaics require the use of mostly opaque glasses and a light box may not be strong enough to illuminate the pattern lines). See *Transferring patterns onto glass* (Basic Techniques, p13–4) for alternative methods.

NOTE Mix concrete outdoors whenever possible. This will prevent the active ingredients and dust in the cement mixture from entering your work area and/or home.

Safety practices

While building a mosaic, there are four items that should always be present and used when appropriate: safety glasses or goggles, work apron, rubber or latex gloves, respirator or dust mask.

The following common sense rules will ensure a safe work environment. NOTE Young children should not work with mosaics unless supervised by an adult. Pregnant women are advised to check with their physician.

1 Always wear safety glasses or goggles when cutting glass. This will prevent the risk of injury to eyes from small glass fragments that may become airborne during cutting.

2 Protect your clothing by wearing a full length work apron at every stage in the mosaic construction process.

3 Wear closed shoes to prevent glass fragments and cement powders from coming in contact with your feet.

4 Premixed mortar cement compounds form a caustic, calcium hydroxide solution when mixed with water. When handling cement powders and wet mixtures, avoid contact with skin or eyes by wearing tight-fitting safety glasses or goggles, rubber or latex gloves, and protective clothing (long-sleeved work shirts and full-length pants are recommended).

5 Wash thoroughly with soap and water, any skin areas and clothing that come in contact with wet cement mixtures or concrete. Wash work clothes and aprons separately from other clothing.

6 Wear a dust mask or respirator when handling or mixing cement and grout powders. For pertinent information on respirators and filters, visit your local safety supply store.

7 Work outdoors, if possible, or in a well ventilated area, especially when mixing cement or working with adhesives. Whenever possible, use adhesives that are nontoxic.

8 Do not eat, drink, or smoke while working with cement and grout dusts and powders. Keep hands away from mouth and face and wash exposed skin areas with soap and water to avoid the possibility of ingesting them.

9 Cover all cuts and scrapes with an adhesive plaster when working with cement or grout to prevent skin irritation.

10 Clean your work area and floor surface with a damp mop or wet sponge to prevent cement and grout powders and dusts from becoming airborne.

11 Carry glass in a vertical position with one hand supporting the sheet from below and the other hand steadying the sheet from the side. Wear protective gloves when moving larger sheets.

Basic Techniques

Selecting glass

The various combinations of color, texture, and light determine the look of a finished mosaic piece. Selecting materials to give the best effect is an interesting and challenging aspect of any project. These guidelines may be helpful.

1 View several selections of glass in lighting conditions similar to those where your finished project will be displayed. Glasses used for a mosaic project should be chosen for their reflective surface qualities and not their ability to transmit light and color.

2 Choose opaque glasses that will obscure the adhesives and cements used to adhere the glass pieces to the base/support structure of the mosaic. If translucent glass is used, keep in mind that any cements, adhesives, or grouts may show through or distort the color of the glass pieces. If a translucent glass is chosen, consider using one with an iridescent finish that reflects light.

3 Vibrant and colorful glass is recommended for mosaic pieces. Larger projects permit the use of more color variations. Smaller projects use 2 or 3 colors. To achieve a wider color range you can vary shades of one of the dominant colors. View glass choices side by side to see how the colors affect each other and consider the color of grout or cement to be used for the project.

4 At least one side of the glass surface must be as smooth as possible for the garden stone projects. If you use glass pieces that are heavily textured they may not stick to the adhesive-backed vinyl and may become partially or completely buried in the cement.

NOTE Amounts of glass listed for individual projects are a close approximation for that pattern. You may wish to purchase more glass to allow for matching glass textures and grain or for possible breakage. Take the pattern with you when purchasing glass from a stained glass retailer.

Copying patterns

Make 2 or 3 copies of the pattern for the project you are working on. Be sure all pattern copies are accurate.

Photocopying This is the easiest method to duplicate copies. Be sure to verify each copy with the original pattern for accuracy. Many photocopiers can also enlarge or reduce patterns.

Tracing Lay tracing vellum over the pattern and trace the lines of the design. You can make more than one copy at a time by using carbon sheets. Lay a sheet of paper on the work surface and place a carbon face down on it. For each additional copy, add another layer of paper and carbon. Place the project pattern on top and fasten in place, using push pins or tape. Trace the outline of the pattern, pressing firmly so that the image is transferred through to each layer of paper.

Grid method Grid work can be used to enlarge, reduce, or change the dimensions of a design. On paper large enough to accommodate the desired size, draw a new grid work with the size of the squares adjusted to fit the new grid. Copy the design from the original grid onto the modified one, square by square. NOTE For sizing reference, patterns in this book that are not full size are placed on grid work (1 square = 1 in or 2.5 cm).

Blueprinting By tracing the project pattern onto drawing vellum, exact copies can be made by a blueprinting firm. Blueprints are exact and do not distort the pattern in any way.

Overhead and opaque projectors Projectors can be used to enlarge pattern designs, but patterns may be distorted and require adjustments. We recommend using this method as a guideline only. When enlarging patterns with pieces that must be a certain size, the pattern will have to be altered accordingly.

Transferring patterns onto glass

For accurate glass cutting draw the outline of the piece to be cut directly onto the glass with a permanent waterproof fine-tipped marker. Try to position the pattern piece on the glass sheet to avoid excessive waste when cutting. Take into account the grain or texture of the glass piece and the flow it will create with the other glass pieces around it. Leave approximately $\frac{1}{4}$ in (0.6 cm) around the piece so the breaking pliers will have some material to grasp when breaking the score line.

For many translucent and light-colored opalescent glasses, the pattern can be transferred by placing the sheet of glass directly on the pattern copy and tracing the design lines with the marker. A light box will help illuminate the pattern from below, but it is not essential.

For opaque glass, the pattern can be transferred onto the glass using one of three methods.

1 Using an extra copy of the pattern, cut out the required pattern piece. Place the pattern piece on the glass and trace around the outside edges with a marker.

2 Make a template from card stock or lightweight cardboard of the pieces to be cut (using the tracing method described on p13) and trace around the template perimeter with the marker, onto the glass. This method is preferable when making several projects using the same pattern.

NOTE When cutting out a piece from the pattern copy or making a cardboard template, be sure to cut on the *inside* of the pattern lines so that the glass piece does not become larger than the pattern once it has been traced and cut.

3 Place a carbon sheet face down on the glass with the pattern on top. By pressing firmly on the lines with a pen or pencil, the pattern will be transferred onto the glass. Go over the carbon lines with the marker.

Cutting glass with a glass cutter

Cutting a piece of glass is the result of two separate actions—scoring and breaking. Once the requisite shape has been traced onto the glass with a permanent waterproof fine-tipped marker, the outline is scored by running the wheel of a glass cutter along the traced line. By applying even pressure on either side of the score line, the piece is broken away from the main sheet of glass.

Cutting glass properly is a skill that can be attained with a little practice. Use 3mm float glass (windowpane glass) to practice cutting flow and amount of pressure to exert. Draw cutting patterns A, B, C, and D (pp16–7) on windowpane glass and practice the techniques of scoring and breaking before starting your first project.

Glass cutting basics

1 Wear safety glasses and a work apron. Stand in an upright position in front of the work table.

2 Work on a clean, level, nonskid work surface covered with newspaper.

3 Place the glass smooth side up, on which the pattern has been traced with the marker. Make sure the surface of the glass is clean and free of any debris.

4 Hold the cutter in your writing hand perpendicular to the glass, not tilted to the left or the right. Run the cutter away from your body and inside the pattern lines, applying steady pressure as you score. The pressure should be coming mainly from your shoulder, not your hand. Lubricate the wheel of the cutter before each score if it is not self-oiling. How you hold the cutter in your hand will depend on what type is used and what grip is the most comfortable.

5 Start and finish the score line at an edge of the glass. Do not stop or lift your cutter from the glass surface before the score is completed. Use a fluid motion, exerting constant, even pressure. Because of their shape, some pieces will require that you make a series of scores and breaks.

6 Never go over a score line a second time. To do so will damage the cutter wheel and increase the likelihood of an unsuccessful break.

7 To complete the break, grasp the

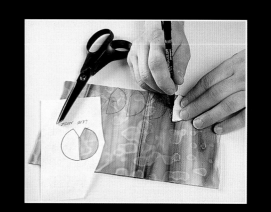

Cut out individual pattern pieces and trace on glass.

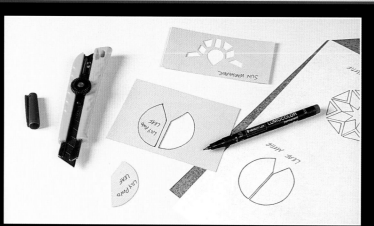

Make a template of each pattern piece and trace on glass. Templates of small intricate sections of pattern borders make easier transfer of pattern to glass.

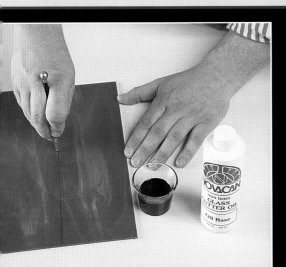

Disposable cutters and oil-fed cutters are held in the traditional manner. The cutter rests between the index and middle fingers with the ball of the thumb placed to push the cutter along. The disposable cutter wheel must be lubricated before each score and wears out quickly.

glass with a hand on each side of the score line, thumbs parallel to the score, knuckles touching. Roll wrists up and outward, breaking the glass along the scored line.

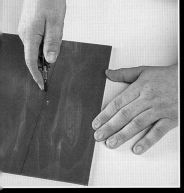

Pistol grip cutter held in palm of hand with the thumb resting on top of the barrel and index finger guiding cutter head.

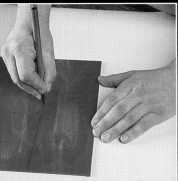

Pencil style cutter, oil-fed, and held as a pencil.

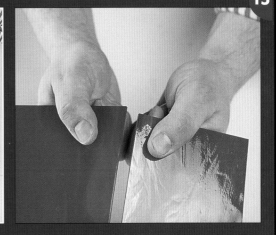

Break glass along the scored line, as shown.

Always start a score line on one edge of the glass and complete the score at another edge.

Practice patterns
full size

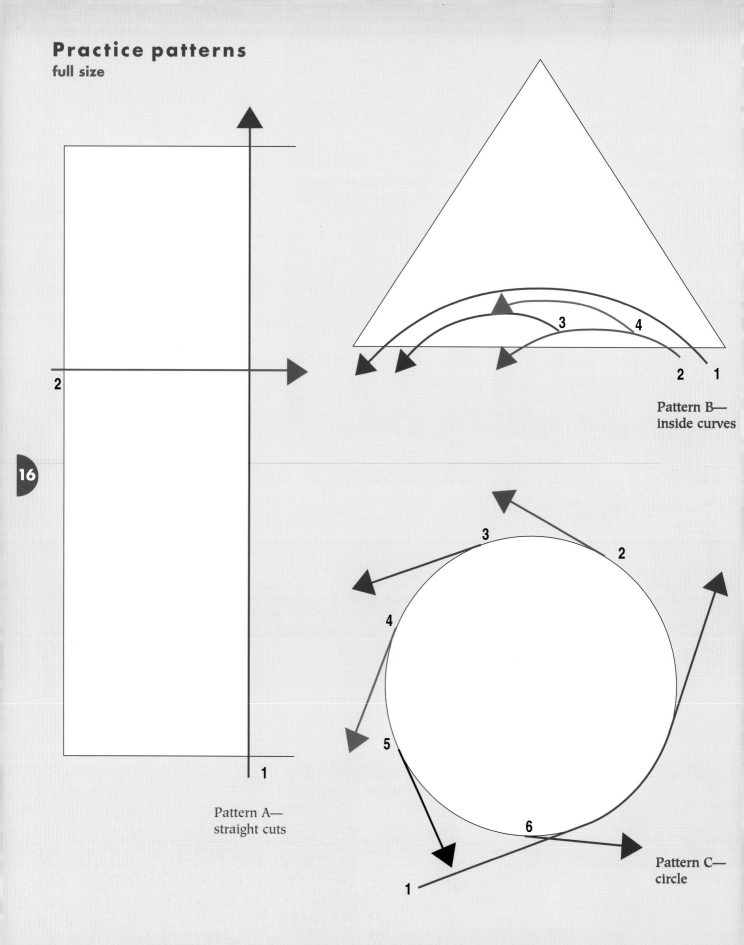

Pattern B—
inside curves

Pattern A—
straight cuts

Pattern C—
circle

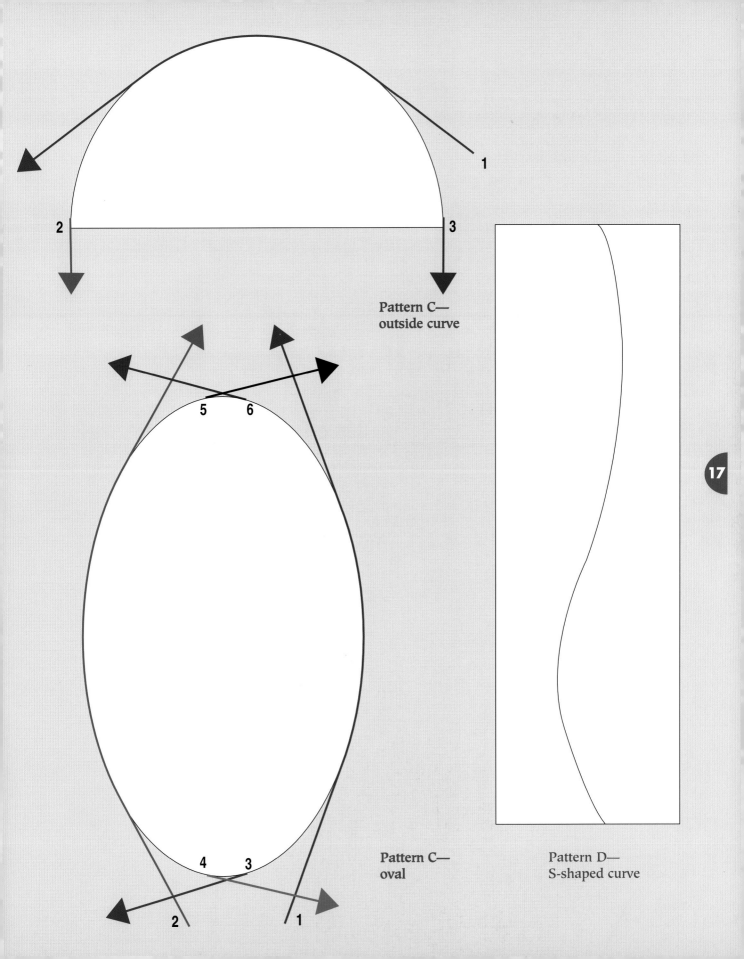

Pattern C—
outside curve

Pattern C—
oval

Pattern D—
S-shaped curve

Breaking glass on a score line

Score lines can also be broken using several different types of pliers designed for the stained glass craft.

Using running pliers For several of the projects in this book, many square and rectangular pieces of glass are required. Running pliers are ideal for breaking straight lines and slight curves and are also useful for starting a break at either end of a score line. Metal running pliers are preferable. The slightly concave jaw must be placed on the topside of the glass and the convex jaw on the underside. If you use plastic running pliers, position the jaw with the two outside "teeth" or ridges on the topside of the glass.

1 Position the running pliers so that the score line is centered and the glass is partially inside the jaws, approximately ½ in to ¾ in (1.3 cm to 1.9 cm).

2 Gently squeeze the handles and the score will "run" (travel), causing the glass to break off into two pieces. If the "run" does not go the full length of the score line, repeat the procedure at the other end of the score line. The two "runs" should meet, causing the score line to break completely.

Using breaking pliers or combination pliers Breaking pliers have two identical flat, smooth jaws that can be placed on either side of the glass. Combination pliers have a flat top jaw and a curved bottom jaw; both are serrated.

1 Position the pliers perpendicular to the score line and as close as possible without touching it. Start at either end of the score line (not the middle).

2 Use an out-and-downward pulling motion on the pliers to break the glass.

3 When using two sets of pliers to

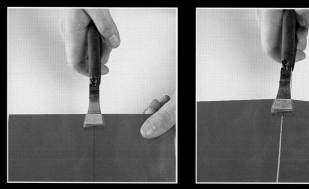

For breaking straight lines or slight curves on glass, use the running pliers.

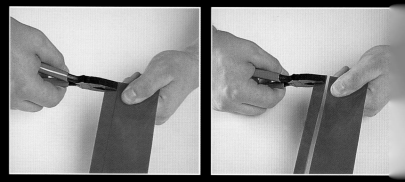

Combination pliers or breaking pliers are positioned perpendicular to the score line.

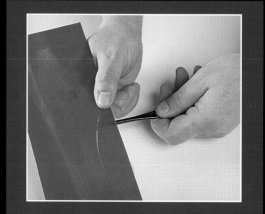

As a last resort, difficult to break glass may be tapped underneath the score line to "urge" the run to begin.

Place the straightedge parallel with the score line.

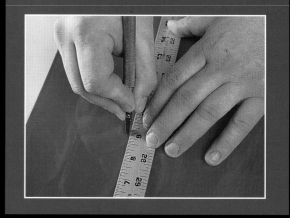

break apart two smaller pieces of glass, place the pliers on the glass on either side of the score line and opposite to each other. Hold one set of pliers steady and use an out-and-downward pulling motion with the other set to separate the glass piece.

Breaking a score line by tapping underneath   Occasionally you may be unable to break a score line using your hands or a set of pliers. Tapping may be required but may cause small chips and fractures along the score line and, if not done carefully, may result in the score running in a different direction than the one intended. The larger the glass piece being cut and the longer the score line, the greater the risk of an unsuccessful break. Tapping should be used only as a last resort.

1 Hold the glass close to the surface of the work table. Using the ball at the end of the cutter, gently strike the glass from the underside, directly underneath the score line. Once the score begins to "run," continue tapping ahead of the "run" until it reaches the other end of the score line.
2 With your hands or a pair of pliers, separate the scored piece from the main sheet of glass.

Scoring a straight line   To score straight lines, the most consistent method is to use a cork-backed metal straightedge.
1 Mark the line to be cut and position the straightedge parallel and approximately ⅛ in (0.3 cm) from the line (the exact distance is determined by the width of the cutter head).
2 Align the head of the glass cutter with the straightedge and verify that the wheel is positioned upon the marked line.
3 Holding the straightedge firmly on the surface of glass, make the score

line by either pulling the cutter toward the body or by pushing it away. Maintain even pressure throughout.
4 Break the score line, using the method you prefer (p18).

Cutting squares and rectangles
Because it is almost impossible to cut glass at a 90° angle, a series of straight scores and breaks is needed when cutting square and rectangular pieces.
1 Trace pattern A (p16) onto the glass, aligning one of the sides of the pattern with the edge of the glass.
2 Score along the other side of the pattern piece and proceed to break the score line, using the method you prefer.
3 Score and break any remaining cut required to achieve the shape of the pattern piece.

Cutting inside curves   Inside curves are the most difficult cuts to score and break out successfully. Attempt the most difficult cut of a piece first, before cutting the piece away from the main sheet of glass.
1 Trace pattern piece B (p16) onto the glass. Position the outer edges of the curve so they align with the edge of the glass.
2 Score the inside curve of the pattern piece but do not attempt to break it out at this time.
3 Make several smaller concave score lines (scallops) between the initial score line and the outside edge of the glass.
4 Using breaker or combination pliers, start removing the scallops, one at a time, beginning with the one closest to the edge of the glass. Use a pulling action with the pliers rather than a downward motion. Remember to position the jaws of the pliers at either end of the score line and not in the middle.

Cutting squares and rectangles requires several straight cuts.

Cutting inside curves requires a series of concave cuts. Attempt the most difficult cut before breaking the piece away from the main sheet of glass.

5 Continue to break away the scallops until you reach the initial score line. Remove it and proceed to score and break away the pattern piece from the larger glass sheet. NOTE The tapping method of running a score line can be used, with care, to break out stubborn pieces.

Cutting circles, ovals, and outside curves

1 Trace pattern C (pp16–7) onto the glass, leaving ½ in (1.3 cm) from the outside edge of the glass.

2 Make an initial score line that will separate the pattern piece from the sheet of glass. The score line will go from the outside edge of the glass and upon reaching the circle will follow the perimeter of it for a short distance and then head off on a tangent to an opposite edge of the glass (see line 1). Break away this piece.

3 The second score line will follow around the circle for a short distance (approximately one-sixth of the perimeter) and then leave on a tangent to the outside edge (see line 2).

4 Repeat step 3, scoring and breaking the glass in a pinwheel fashion, until the circle shape has been formed (see lines 3, 4, 5, and 6).

5 Small jagged edges where a score line was started or ended can be ground off with a glass grinder, filed off with a carborundum stone, or nibbled away with combination pliers (see Grozing, p21).

6 This method for cutting circular pieces can be adapted to cut outside curves and ovals.

Scoring and breaking S-shaped curves

1 Trace pattern D (p17) onto the glass, placing one of the sides against the edge of the glass.

20

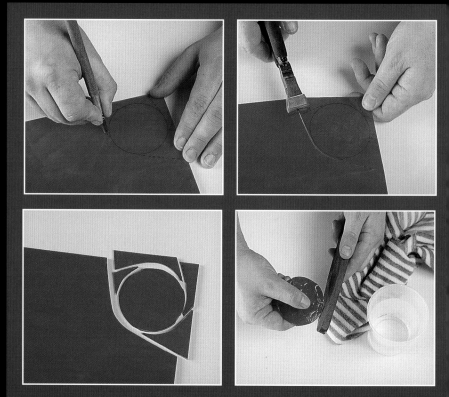

A series of breaks following the arrows on pattern C on pages 16 and 17 will create circular and oval shapes.

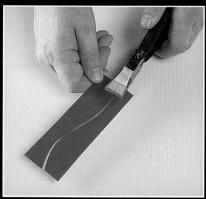

S-shaped curves require starting "runs" at each end of the score line so the runs meet near the center.

Jagged edges of glass can be smoothed by grozing.

2 Score the most difficult cut first (S-shape).

3 Align the running pliers with the score line. Squeeze only hard enough to start the "run." Repeat the procedure at the opposite end of the score line. If both "runs" meet, use your hands to separate the resulting two pieces. If the "runs" do not meet, gently tap along the score line (on the underside of the glass).

4 Score and break out remaining cuts.

Grozing

The jagged edge of the glass along the broken out score line can be smoothed by grozing. Grasping the piece of glass firmly in one hand, place the combination pliers perpendicular to the edge of the glass and drag the serrated jaws along the jagged edge in an up-and-down motion. Repeat until the edge is smooth.

Cutting glass using glass mosaic cutters

Glass mosaic cutters, also known as nippers, can be used to cut and shape many of the smaller pieces required to complete a glass mosaic project.

1 Using a glass cutter and pliers, cut a strip or piece of glass from a larger sheet, slightly larger than the pattern piece that you require.

2 With a permanent waterproof fine-tipped marker, trace the outline of the pattern piece onto the glass.

3 Grip the mosaic cutters in your writing hand and hold the glass in the opposite hand. Using a scissors-like motion, nip away portions of glass along the trace line until you have achieved the desired shape.

NOTE Always wear safety glasses when using any glass cutting or breaking tool.

Cutting stained glass tesserae

For many of the projects in this book, a number of square or rectangular pieces are required to fill in certain areas. In traditional mosaic works, a small piece of colored glass used in this manner is known as a tessera (*pl.* tesserae). Two methods are described below for making stained glass tesserae.

Cutting uniform tesserae

1 Cut a piece of glass 12 in x 12 in (30.5 cm x 30.5 cm), making sure that the edges are square.

2 Align a ruler along one side of the sheet of glass and make a mark on the edge of the glass at every 1 in (2.5 cm) interval.

3 Repeat step 2 on each of the four sides of the glass sheet.

4 Align a cork-backed straightedge along the marks on two opposite sides and score a straight line at each 1 in (2.5 cm) interval with a glass cutter.

5 Repeat step 4 for the remaining two sides. There should be a grid work of score lines visible on the surface of the glass.

6 With a pair of running pliers, break the score lines along one side, creating strips 1 in (2.5 cm) wide x 12 in (30.5 cm) long.

7 Take each strip and break the remaining score lines. There should now be 12 dozen 1 in (2.5 cm) pieces.

NOTE To make tesserae of varying amounts and sizes, simply adjust the size of the glass sheet and the intervals at which the sheet is to be scored.

Cutting random-size tesserae

1 With a glass cutter, randomly score lines from one edge of a small sheet of glass to the opposite side. Try to

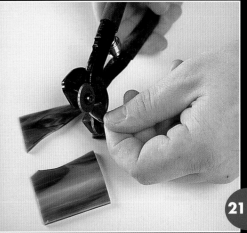

21

Nippers are one of the most popular tools for making tesserae. The shapes are not always even—in character with the art of stained glass mosaics.

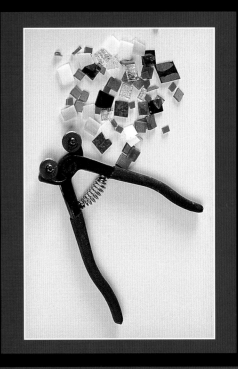

vary the width between each score line while keeping the score lines no wider than 1 in (2.5 cm) apart.

2 Repeat step 1 for the remaining two opposite sides.

3 With a pair of running pliers, break the score lines along one side, creating long narrow strips.

4 Take each strip and break the remaining score lines into individual, random-size pieces.

NOTE An alternative method is to cut narrow strips and then proceed to nip the strips into smaller various size pieces with a pair of glass mosaic cutters.

Smoothing jagged edges of glass

The fun of creating a mosaic is that its pieces do not need to fit the pattern as precisely as is required when constructing a stained glass window. However, if edges are too jagged they can be smoothed away and pieces can be shaped with a glass grinder. If less smoothing is required, a carborundum stone is all that you need. If you cannot cut the glass into the shape required and you do not have access to a glass grinder, alter the pattern to accommodate the shape that you can achieve.

NOTE Always wear safety glasses and a work apron whenever a glass grinder or carborundum stone is used to work with glass.

Using a carborundum stone

Carborundum stones (small rectangular block composed of a hard carbon compound and silicon) are available at most hardware stores.

1 Wet the carborundum stone and the piece of glass with water. The stone must be wet at all times to help keep minute glass particles and dust from becoming airborne.

2 Rub the stone, in a file-like motion, along the edge of the glass that

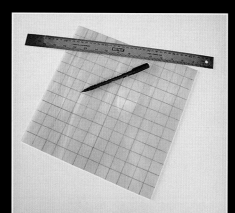

Cutting uniform 1 in (2.5 cm) tesserae requires making a grid on the glass and scoring with a glass cutter and a straightedge.

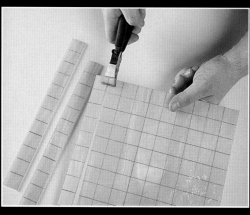

Running pliers break the scored lines into strips.

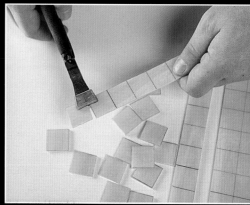

Break strips into individual tesserae.

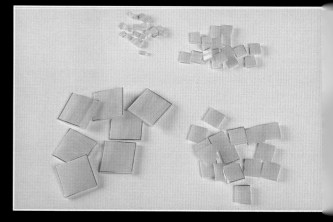

To make tesserae of varying amounts and sizes, simply adjust the size of the glass sheet and the intervals at which the sheet is to be scored.

requires smoothing.

3 Rinse the glass and the carborundum stone under running water to wash away glass residue.

Using a glass grinder

1 Have a face shield attached to the grinder and position a backsplash along the back and sides of the grinder to contain any airborne glass chips and water overspray.

2 Keep water in the reservoir and have a moistened sponge positioned adjacent to the diamond-coated bit at all times.

3 Cut each glass piece on the inside of the pattern line to fit the pattern with a minimum of grinding and to allow for cement or grout to fit between each piece. If the glass pieces fit the pattern and you are concerned about sharp edges, make one quick swipe against the grinding bit on each edge of the glass to dull any sharpness. Only light pressure is required when pushing the glass against the bit.

4 If traces of the marked line are still visible on the piece, grind the edge to ensure an accurate fit within the pattern lines.

5 Check each piece against the pattern. If any part of the piece overlaps and there is not adequate spacing between the pattern pieces, mark the area with a permanent waterproof marker and grind away the excess.

6 Rinse each piece under clear running water when grinding is complete.

7 Ensure proper performance of the glass grinder by cleaning thoroughly and rinsing the water reservoir after each use.

Remember to keep the carborundum stone wet at all times when it is being used. Rinse away glass residue when finished.

For those who have a glass grinder, follow the manufacturer's instructions for using your grinder. A swipe along the edges of the glass will take away any sharp edges.

23

Check each piece against the pattern. Mark areas needing further grinding and continue to grind away excess glass until the piece fits inside the pattern lines.

SAFETY REMINDER Always wear safety glasses or goggles and a work apron. Work with nontoxic adhesives whenever possible and always in a well ventilated room. When mixing dry grout powders, wear a respirator or dust mask to avoid inhaling airborne particles. Wear rubber or latex gloves to protect hands when grouting mosaic projects.

Stained Glass Mosaic Decorative Projects

Stained glass mosaic has exploded in popularity in the past few years and today it is one of the leading crafts chosen by hobbyists. Besides producing decorative and useful objects, mosaic pieces using art glass are easy to do, look beautiful, and the equipment needed to pursue the craft is found in the home workshop or is available at local supply stores. Stained glass comes in a wide selection of decorative colors and is easily cut into appropriate sizes to make any of the patterns in this book, from planters to tabletops to mirror frames to birdbaths. Choose any project and create a decorative mosaic to accent your home or garden.

Construction Techniques

Direct Method

Materials
2 copies of pattern
Base or support structure for mosaic
Carbon paper
Masking tape
Newspaper
Glass pieces for project
Dish soap and water
Tile adhesive
Paper cup
Tile grout
Water

Tools
Apron
Safety glasses
Utility knife
Hard-tipped pen or pencil
Permanent waterproof fine-tipped
  marker
Cork-backed straightedge
Glass cutter
Glass mosaic nippers
Running pliers
Breaking/grozing pliers
Carborundum stone or glass grinder
Small containers or jars
Craft stick or small palette knife
Tweezers
Paint scraper
Small container for mixing grout
Respirator or dust mask
Rubber or latex gloves
Sponge
Soft cloth
Soft bristled brushes and/or
  toothbrush

Preparing the pattern
1 Make 2 copies (p13) of the chosen pattern.
2 Verify that the outline of the pattern fits within the designated area on the object to be covered. If you adjust the pattern to ensure a better fit, be sure to adjust both copies.
3 Use one copy as a guide for cutting and breaking the glass pieces to the correct size and shape. Use the second copy to cut out any pattern piece for which a template is required (when cutting opaque glass), remembering to cut inside the pattern lines. *See p14.*

Transferring the pattern onto the base or support structure
1 Make sure the support/base structure is clean and free of debris.
2 Place a sheet of carbon paper onto the base/support structure, over the area to be covered with the glass mosaic pieces. Trim the carbon to fit if the surface is not flat. Fasten with masking tape.
3 Position a copy of the pattern on top of the carbon, making sure it is in the correct position. Fasten with masking tape.
4 Trace the pattern lines onto the base/support structure with a hard tipped pen or pencil.
5 Key (rough up by scoring with a utility knife) the surface of a wood base/support structure at the place where the glass pieces are to be adhered. Small cuts into the wood surface will be sufficient. Do not gouge the wood.

Preparing the glass pieces
1 Use the pattern copies and a marker to trace (pp13–4) each pattern piece onto the glass to be cut. You do not need to trace each of the numerous tesserae of the same size and shape required for a project. Each pattern requiring these pieces will specify the size and number of pieces to cut.
2 Cut (pp14-22) each piece of glass required, making sure to cut inside

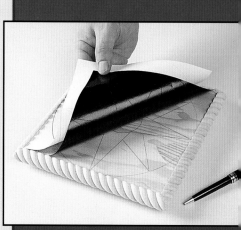

After verifying that the pattern fits properly, transfer the pattern onto the base/support structure using carbon paper.

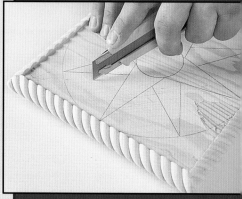

The surface of the base/support structure must be roughened up to ensure the adhesives will hold the tesserae to the structure.

the marker line. Use the cork-backed straightedge to assist in scoring straight lines (p19) and tesserae (p21).

3 Smooth or grind any glass edges that are jagged or do not fit the pattern (pp22–3). Glass mosaic construction does not demand the precision needed to make a stained glass window. The pieces should fit inside the pattern lines. The spacing created by the width of the design lines allows the grout to get in and around the individual pieces for a smoother finish and a better bond to the project.

4 Clean each piece thoroughly to ensure adhesion to the base/support structure. Remove all traces of cutter oil, marker, grinding residue, etc. with soap and water. Rinse thoroughly with clean water.

5 Separate tesserae by size and color and store in small jars or containers until ready for use.

Adhering the glass pieces to the base/support structure

1 Protect areas that are not to be covered with adhesive or grout with masking tape before adhering the glass pieces to the base/support structure. This will aid in the final clean up.

2 Choose a ceramic tile adhesive that is appropriate for the project. For pieces that will be placed outdoors, select waterproof or water-resistant tile adhesive. Follow the manufacturer's instructions.

3 Mix in a bit of the grout to tint the adhesive if the grout (to be used in the next stage) differs in color from the adhesive. This will make it less noticeable wherever adhesive oozes up between the glass pieces and cannot be removed or covered with grout.

4 Work with a small amount of adhesive in a paper cup (most are premixed and ready for application). Keep the rest of the adhesive in the closed container so it will not be exposed to air and start to harden. Replenish cup as needed.

5 Use a craft stick or small palette knife to spread a layer of adhesive onto the back of a glass piece. This is called "buttering."

6 Press the glass piece firmly onto the base/support structure in the correct position. There should be just enough adhesive on the back of the piece so that on placement a small amount oozes out from underneath and around the bottom edges of the glass piece.

7 Start with the main design elements and specific glass shapes in the pattern when adhering the glass pieces to the base/support structure. Applying the glass pieces color by color also helps to avoid mix-ups in the placement.

8 Fill in the background of the project with the remaining tesserae until all areas of the mosaic pattern have been covered. *See* photos. For areas of the mosaic that are to be filled with a number of the same type of tesserae, apply a layer of the adhesive directly onto the base/support structure surface and

If grout color and adhesive color do not match, mix a bit of grout with the adhesive in case the adhesive oozes out from beneath the tesserae.

Butter main elements of the piece. Pressing down firmly will cause some adhesive to ooze out around the piece.

Three methods of applying background fill

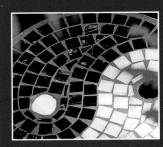

Opus vermiculatum
Tesserae are positioned following the outline of glass pieces already laid. This allows images and lines in the pattern to be accentuated and creates some interesting effects.

Opus tesselatum Similarly sized and shaped tesserae are applied in rows, both horizontally and vertically, in a grid pattern to form an unobtrusive background for the main features of the mosaic.

Random
As the term implies, the pieces are various sizes and shapes and are placed randomly to fill the background area of the mosaic.

press the tesserae firmly in place. This will save buttering each individual tessera and will take less time.

9 Pick up any glass piece that needs adjusting with the aid of a pair of tweezers or a utility knife if it is not in the correct position. Apply additional adhesive, if required, and reset the piece in the mosaic.

10 Allow the adhesive to set for 24 hours or as recommended by the adhesive manufacturer.

11 Use a utility knife or paint scraper to remove any adhesive that may have gotten onto the surface of the glass pieces after the adhesive has set. Take care not to scratch the surface of the glass.

Applying the grout

Determine whether you prefer sanded or non-sanded grout to finish off the project. Sanded grout is grainier and suitable for outdoor projects and terra-cotta pots. Non-sanded grouts have a smooth finish but have a tendency to shrink so additional coats of grout may be necessary to fill in the spaces between the glass pieces. Use waterproof or water-resistant grouts for finished outdoor pieces or for pots that may come in contact with a lot of moisture.

1 Mix the required amount of dry grout with water in a small container, in accordance with the manufacturer's instructions.

2 Begin to apply the grout to the mosaic's surface with a damp sponge or with your gloved hand. Gently work it in between the glass pieces until the grout is flush with the surface of the glass and all crevices are filled.

3 Wipe excess grout off the surface of the glass mosaic with a water-dampened sponge and smooth the top of grouted areas level with the glass pieces.

4 Allow to dry following the manufacturer's instructions. Some grouts require that a damp cloth be placed over the mosaic so that the grout will not dry too quickly and crack.

Cleaning the finished piece

Once the grout is completely dry, clean the surface of the finished glass mosaic by buffing with a soft cloth. A soft bristled brush can be used to rub off excess grout. Use a paint scraper or utility knife to scrape away any remaining grout or adhesive. Finally, remove any masking material.

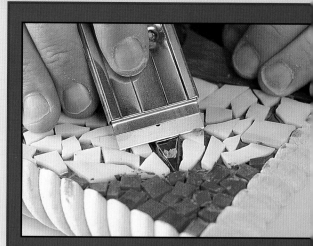

Allow adhesive to set for 24 hours. Use a utility knife to remove adhesive on top of tesserae. Be careful not to scratch surface.

The consistency of the grout is very important—not too runny, but not too stiff. With gloves on, gently work the grout between the glass pieces. Wipe excess grout off the surface.

Use a soft cloth to buff the cleaned surface of the mosaic.

Indirect or Reverse Method

Materials

3 copies of pattern
Base or support structure for mosaic
Masking tape
Clear adhesive-backed vinyl
Newspaper
Glass pieces for project
Dish soap and water
Tile adhesive
Cardboard
Clear glass sheet
Flat wooden block
Tile grout
Water

Tools

Apron
Safety glasses
Light table (optional)
Permanent waterproof fine-tipped
    marker
Cork-backed straightedge
Glass cutter
Glass mosaic nippers
Running pliers
Breaking/grozing pliers
Carborundum stone or glass grinder
Small containers or jars
Tweezers
Utility knife
Trowel
Paint scraper
Respirator or dust mask
Rubber or latex gloves
Sponge
Soft cloth
Soft bristled brushes and/or
    toothbrush

Preparing the pattern

1 Make 3 copies (p13) of the pattern you have chosen.

2 Verify that the outline of the pattern fits within the designated area of the object to be covered. If you adjust the pattern to ensure a better fit, be sure to adjust the other two copies as well.

3 Use one copy as a guide for cutting and breaking the glass pieces to the correct size and shape. Use the second copy to cut out any pattern piece for which a template is required (when cutting opaque glass), remembering to cut inside the pattern lines (p14). Use the third copy to place beneath the clear adhesive-backed vinyl to act as a guide when laying out the glass pieces for the glass mosaic panel.

4 Place a pattern copy face down on a light table and trace the design lines onto the reverse side with the marker. If a light table is not available, tape the pattern onto a window (with the design facing outside), and trace.

5 Tape the pattern copy to a flat work surface or board, with the reverse side facing upward.

6 Peel the paper backing from a piece of clear adhesive-backed vinyl that is approximately ½ in (1.3 cm) larger on each side than the project pattern. Position the vinyl over the pattern taped to work surface, with the adhesive side facing upwards. Do not stick it to the pattern. The vinyl should be centered so that approximately ½ in (1.3 cm) of vinyl overlaps the pattern on each side. The pattern should be completely covered by the vinyl yet visible through it. Tape in place, taking care not to position tape within the pattern outline.

NOTE Use clear 8 mil sandblast resist material for the strength of its adhesive and the thickness of the vinyl. It is available through most stained glass stores. As an alternative, use clear contact paper that can be purchased at most department and hardware stores. However, the adhesive of contact paper is not as good and the glass pieces may not stick to it as well as to the resist.

Preparing the glass pieces

Follow the instructions for this stage given in Direct Method (pp26–7). As listed in step 4, each piece must be cleaned thoroughly to ensure adhesion to the clear adhesive-backed vinyl.

The adhesive-backed vinyl should be larger than the pattern. Position over pattern, adhesive side up. Tape pattern and vinyl to work surface.

Placing the glass pieces onto the vinyl

You are now ready to place your cut glass pieces onto the clear adhesive-backed vinyl. Remember, the pattern copy under the vinyl is the reverse of the pattern you have used to cut the glass pieces.

1 Start with the main design elements in the project foreground. Turn each glass piece over and place face down onto the vinyl in the correct position. Press the pieces firmly onto the resist.

2 Fill in the background of the project, using one of the methods described on p27, with the remaining tesserae until all areas of the project pattern have been covered.

3 Adjust any glass pieces not in the correct position. Pick up the piece that needs adjusting with the aid of a pair of tweezers or a utility knife. Although the ability to shift or replace a piece of glass is an advantage of working with the indirect method, repeated lifting of pieces from the vinyl may deteriorate the adhesive.

4 Use a utility knife to cut along the outside of the pattern outline and remove excess vinyl.

5 Split the mosaic piece into several sections for sizable projects to make application to the base/support structure easier. Being careful not to dislodge any glass pieces, run the blade of the utility knife between the glass pieces and cut the vinyl underneath. Separate into the desired number of sections.

Preparing the base or support structure

1 Make sure the base/support structure is clean and free of debris before you begin.

2 Mark the base/support structure with the pattern outline as a guide to where the mosaic is to be adhered.

3 Key (rough up) the surface of wood support structures by scoring with a utility knife. Small cuts in the wood surface will be sufficient to aid the adhering process. Do not gouge the wood. *See photo, p26.*

Place the main elements of the mosaic first. Fill in the background last. Trim away excess vinyl when all pieces are down.

For ease of handling, split large patterns into sections prior to applying to the base/support structure.

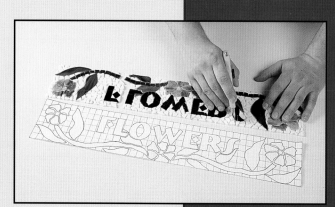

Applying the adhesive

1 Follow steps 1 to 3 from *Adhering the glass pieces to the base/support structure* given in Direct Method (p27).

2 Use a trowel to apply a thin, even layer of adhesive to the base/support structure where the mosaic is to be applied. Try not to cover the outside pattern line because it will act as a guide for applying the glass mosaic.

Adhesive is applied with a trowel in the Indirect Method.

For smaller sections, align one edge of the mosaic section with the corresponding pattern edge. Turn vinyl over and place pieces onto the adhesive.

For larger sections, use cardboard and a sheet of glass that is slightly larger than the mosaic to turn the pieces over. Be sure the glass sheet is not touching the adhesive.

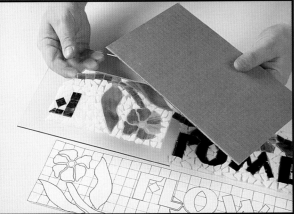

Applying the glass mosaic

The trick to the indirect method is turning over the sections of mosaic that are adhered to the vinyl without dislodging the glass pieces and then applying it to the base/support structure in the correct position.

1 For smaller mosaic sections carefully turn over the sections following these steps.

• With the base/support structure close at hand, gently lift the glass-laden vinyl.

• Align one edge of the mosaic section with the corresponding pattern edge.

• Turn the vinyl over and place the mosaic pieces onto the adhesive. Check that the mosaic section is correctly positioned and press into place.

For larger mosaic sections turn over the sections following these steps.

• Slide the vinyl (with the attached glass pieces) onto a piece of cardboard and place a clear glass sheet (at least 3mm thick) on top. Both the cardboard and the glass sheet must be slightly larger than the mosaic section.

• Hold the layers tightly together, then turn the mosaic section over so that the clear glass sheet is now on the bottom. Remove the top cardboard layer.

• Align the mosaic section with two adjacent edges of the glass sheet. Hold the glass sheet over the base/support structure and line up the edges of the mosaic section with the area where it is to be applied. The glass sheet must not be touching the adhesive.

• Grasp the edges of the vinyl once you are sure of the alignment. With the aid of a helper, pull the clear glass sheet out from beneath the glass mosaic. Press firmly to the adhesive.

31

- Repeat for each mosaic section that is to be adhered. Align each section so that there is not a visible seam or division between them. The mosaic should look like one unit and not a series of ill-fitting sections.

2 Do not remove the vinyl at this stage. Some glass pieces may come away with the vinyl if it is peeled off before the adhesive has set.

3 Using a flat wood block, press the sections down onto the adhesive until they are firmly in place.

4 Allow the adhesive to set for 24 hours or as recommended by the manufacturer.

5 Remove the vinyl, exposing the top side of the glass mosaic. Use a utility knife or paint scraper to remove any adhesive that may have gotten onto the surface of the glass pieces. Take care not to scratch the surface of the glass.

Applying the grout and cleaning the finished piece

Follow the same instructions for these final stages as provided in the Direct Method (p28).

A flat wood block firmly presses glass in place. Allow adhesive to set for 24 hours. Then carefully peel away the vinyl backing.

Making wood base/support structures

This book contains instructions and several patterns for constructing glass mosaic trivets and wall hangings. Although there are many ready-made objects available that can be used for base/support structures, you can make your own very easily. You need only a few woodworking tools and the knowledge to use them safely. If you do not have the necessary skills and tools, perhaps a friend could help.

NOTE When operating power tools, read the manufacturer's directions and follow all safety guidelines and precautions. Always wear an apron and safety glasses.

Trivets and wall hangings
Materials
1 copy of pattern
¾ in (1.9 cm) plywood
Wood trim molding (at least ¾ in or 1.9 cm wide)
Carpenter's wood glue
Finishing nails
Wood filler
Sandpaper
Wood stain
Felt or cork pads

Tools
Apron
Safety glasses
Marking pen or pencil
Drawing or carpenter's square
Wood saw (hand or power)
Hammer or air nailer
Applicator brush for wood stain
Soft cloths for buffing

1 Measure the width and height of the project pattern.
2 Use a marking pen, square, and straightedge, to mark the dimensions required for the base piece onto the plywood sheet, making sure that it is

square. Example: for the 16 in x 16 in (40.6 cm x 40.6 cm) square Sunflower wall hanging (p52), a 16 in x 16 in (40.6 cm x 40.6 cm) square plywood base is required.

3 Cut the base piece away from the main sheet of plywood, using a wood saw.

4 Cut a length of wood trim molding for each of the four sides of the base piece and miter each end at a 45° angle.

5 Apply a bead of carpenter's wood glue to an outside edge of the base piece and place a length of the molding overtop. Fasten the molding to the base piece with a hammer and finishing nails. Repeat this step with the remaining three lengths of trim, making sure that the mitered ends of each length are butted up against the adjacent pieces. The wood trim should be slightly wider than the base piece so that a raised edge is present around the outside perimeter of the base piece. This will give the project a finished look and contain the glass mosaic pieces so they do not stick out over the edge.

6 Fill nail holes and gaps with wood filler and smooth with sandpaper.

7 Finish the exposed wood frame with a complementary colored stain once the glass mosaic pieces have been adhered to the base and the grouting has been completed.

8 Apply felt or cork pads to the bottom of the base piece for trivets to protect table and counter surfaces.

NOTE Use ¾ in (1.9 cm) plywood for base/support structures because of its strength and durability. Plywood will support the weight of a glass mosaic and will not warp.

Wall mirror

Material
1 copy of pattern
¾ in (1.9 cm) plywood
1 in x 4 in (2.5 cm x 10.1 cm) framing lumber
Carpenter's wood glue
No.8 wood screws (1 in or 2.5 cm in length)
Wood trim molding (at least 1⅝ in or 4.1 cm wide)
Finishing nails
Wood filler
Sandpaper
Wood stain

Tools
Apron
Safety glasses
Marking pen or pencil
Drawing or carpenter's square
Wood saw (hand or power)
Power drill with drill bits suitable for woodworking
Hammer or air nailer
Applicator brush for wood stain
Soft cloths for buffing

1 Use a plywood base piece 18 in x 30 in (45.7 cm x 76.2 cm) for the wall mirror back.

2 Cut the 1 in x 4 in (2.5 cm x 10.1 cm) framing lumber into 4 lengths—two 18 in (45.7 cm) lengths and two 30 in (76.2 cm) lengths. Miter each end of the lengths at a 45° angle.
NOTE 1 in x 4 in (2.5 cm x 10.1 cm) framing lumber is actually ¾ in x 3½ in (1.9 cm x 8.9 cm).

3 Bring the mitered ends together to form the four lengths into a frame. Use the square to verify that the four corners are true.

4 Apply carpenter's wood glue to the framework. Position the plywood base on top of the framework and fasten in place with

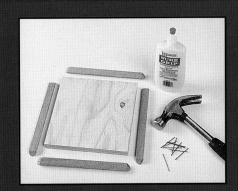

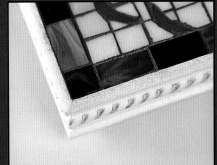

Wood base/support structure for a trivet—note the finished mosaic does not protrude above the framing.

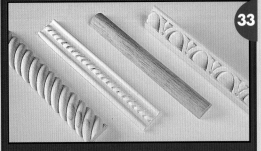

There is a wide variety of framing materials available today.

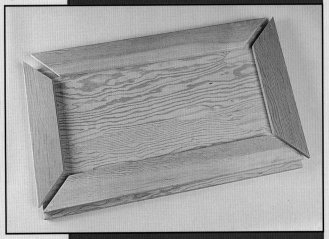

The components of a wall mirror.

The frame is screwed in from the back of the mirror. Countersink screws to prevent scratches on wall.

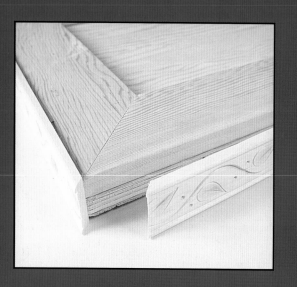

Side trim is applied to cover the plywood backing and top frame seam.

the wood screws. Use at least 3 screws per side. To prevent marring of wall surfaces, countersink the screws so they are level with the plywood surface or place felt or cork pads over the screw heads.

5 Follow steps 4 to 7 given in *Making wood base/support structures—Trivets and wall hangings* (p33). Because of the thickness of the base piece and the attached framework, the molding should be at least 1⅝ in (4.1 cm) wide.

NOTE The glass mosaic is built on the 3½ in (8.9 cm) wide framework. The recessed area for the mirrored glass is approximately 11 in x 23 in (27.9 cm x 58.4 cm).

Mounting wall hangings and mirrors

Glass mosaic wall hangings and mirrors can be hung easily in the location of your choice.

1 Place the wall hanging or mirror face down onto the work surface so that the back of the piece is being viewed.

2 Make two opposite and level marks approximately 1½ in to 2 in (3.8 cm x 5 cm) in from either side. These marks should be placed

approximately 4 in (10.1 cm) from the top of the finished mosaic piece.

3 Fasten an eye screw or a heavy duty eyelet to the plywood base at each of these marks. Use screws that are approximately ½ in (1.3 cm) in length so that they do not go through the ¾ in (1.9 cm) plywood base and damage the mosaic on the front.

4 String a double strand of picture hanging wire between the two screws, threading it through the eyes. Wrap the ends of the wire around the strand to secure it in place.

5 Hang larger and heavier pieces by drilling two holes into the wall in the desired location. Insert the appropriate plugs or anchors, depending on the type of wall surface. Insert and tighten a screw three quarters of the way into each plug. Suspend the mosaic piece on the wall by hooking the wire onto the two screws. A picture hook or small nail will be sufficient to hang small mosaic pieces.

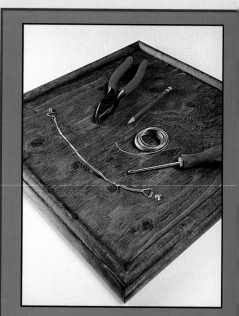

This is one suggestion for mounting wall hangings or mirrors. Remember, the mosaic piece will be heavy and appropriate precautions should be made to ensure the piece does not fall away from the wall.

Flowers & Herbs
planter boxes

Dress up a planter box with glass mosaic design and
fill it with flowers or herbs to beautify your patio or
garden. Cedar planter boxes come in many shapes
and sizes at your local home and garden center. For
those hobbyists with the tools and know-how,
making your own planter can add to the fun.

FLOWERS PLANTER BOX

Approximate number of pieces   600

A   12 in x 12 in (30.5 cm x 30.5 cm) iridescent white (cut into random-size tesserae)

B   5 in x 9 in (12.7 cm x 22.8 cm) dark green and white wispy

C   2 in x 5 in (5 cm x 12.7 cm) dark green, brown and white opaque streaky (cut into ⁵⁄₁₆ in x ⁵⁄₁₆ in or 0.8 cm x 0.8 cm tesserae)

D   5 in x 6 in (12.7 cm x 15.2 cm) black (cut into ⁹⁄₁₆ in x ⁹⁄₁₆ in or 1.4 cm x 1.4 cm tesserae)

E   4 in x 9 in (10.1 cm x 22.8 cm) light purple and royal purple opaque

F   2 in x 2 in (5 cm x 5 cm) yellow and white wispy

HERBS PLANTER BOX

Approximate number of pieces   475

A   12 in x 12 in (30.5 cm x 30.5 cm) iridescent pink and white wispy (cut a 9 in x 12 in or 22.8 cm x 30.5 cm portion of this glass into ½ in x ½ in or 1.3 cm x 1.3 cm tesserae)

B   6 in x 8 in (15.2 cm x 20.3 cm) dark green and white wispy

C   1 in x 3 in (2.5 cm x 7.6 cm) dark green, brown and white opaque streaky (cut into ¼ in x ¼ in or 0.6 cm x 0.6 cm tesserae)

D   3 in x 9 in (7.6 cm x 22.8 cm) black (cut into ⁹⁄₁₆ in x ⁹⁄₁₆ in or 1.4 cm x 1.4 cm tesserae)

1 Construct the mosaic panels for this project by following the instructions given for Indirect or Reverse Method (pp29–32). Refer below to *Special Instructions* for additional steps and information.

2 The side panels on the cedar planter box used in this project are 23 in wide x 4¼ in high x ⁹⁄₁₆ in thick (58.4 cm x 10.8 cm x 1.4 cm). The pattern for the glass mosaic has been made ¹⁄₁₆ in (0.15 cm) smaller on each of the four sides, leaving a slight allowance for any variance in size of the wood panels or thickness of the glass pieces. Any size planter can be used if the pattern is adjusted accordingly.

3 If the planter is to be left outdoors, treat the wood with a water-resistant sealer before starting the project. Select waterproof or water-resistant tile adhesives and grout.

Special Instructions

Placing the glass pieces onto the vinyl

1 Follow steps 1 to 5 (p30).

NOTE   Because of the project width,

separate the mosaic piece into three sections before adhering to the planter side panel. Each section should be approximately 8 in (20.3 cm) wide. *See* p30.

Applying the glass mosaic

1 Follow steps 1 to 5 (pp31–2).

2 Give the project a more finished look by using tesserae (made of the same glass as the mosaic background) to cover the exposed wood edges on the top and either side of the glass mosaic. Measure the thickness of the wood panel now that the glass mosaic has been adhered. The side panel is now approximately ⅝ in (1.6 cm) thick.

3 The background tesserae for the Herb project are ½ in x ½ in (1.3 cm x 1.3 cm) squares (*opus tesselatum*, p27); however, wider tesserae will be required to cover the exposed wood and mosaic edge. Cut enough ½ in x ⅝ in (1.3 cm x 1.6 cm) rectangular tesserae to cover the top and side edges. The background method for the Flower project is random (p27).

4 With a small palette knife, apply a

thin, even layer of the adhesive to the exposed edges. Apply the tesserae, aligning each individual tessera with the adjacent piece on the glass mosaic panel. See the photograph of the finished planter (p35).

5 Allow the adhesive to set for 24 hours or as recommended by the manufacturer.

Complete the project by following the instructions for *Applying the grout* and *Cleaning the finished piece* (p28).

HELPFUL HINT   When smaller tesserae (¼ in x ¼ in or 0.6 cm x 0.6 cm) are required for a project, it is often easier to cut a larger size tessera into a few pieces of the smaller size. Use the glass mosaic cutters (nippers) or a glass cutter to divide a tessera in half and from there into smaller shapes and sizes.

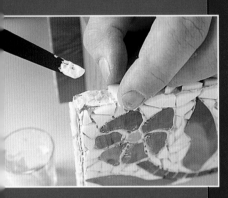

For a more finished look, apply tesserae to the exposed wood edges on the top and either side of the planter box.

Use the nippers to make very small tesserae from larger sizes.

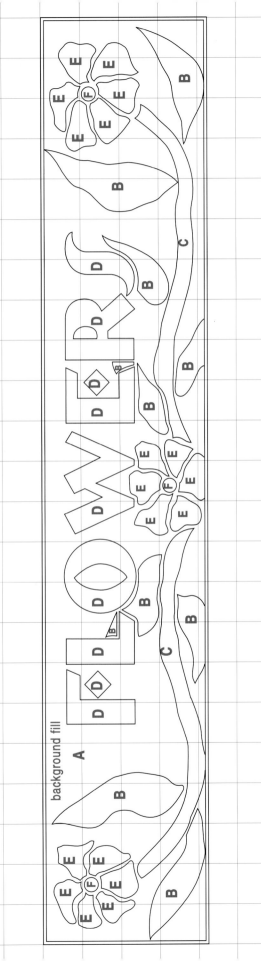

background fill

background fill

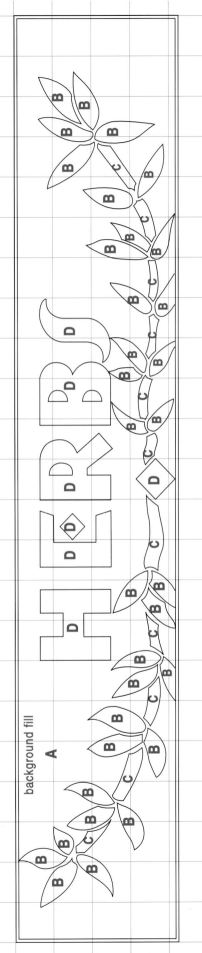

Snakes & Lizards cactus pots

Celebrate the sun with a desert setting right in your own garden. This Southwest motif of slithering snakes and sun-drenched lizards on earthy terra-cotta containers is ideal for a wide variety of cacti. Make as many lizard pots and snake pots as you need, then arrange them to show off your garden creation.

SNAKES CACTUS POT

Approximate number of pieces   123 plus background tesserae

A   3 in x 4 in (7.6 cm x 10.1 cm) iridescent white (cut into ½ in x ½ in or 1.3 cm x 1.3 cm tesserae)

B   3 in x 4 in (7.6 cm x 10.1 cm) black (cut into ½ in x ½ in or 1.3 cm x 1.3 cm tesserae)

C   1 in x 1 in (2.5 cm x 2.5 cm) red and white wispy

D   2 in x 2 in (5 cm x 5 cm) brown and amber opaque

E   iridescent white glass nugget (small)

F   2 in x 4 in (5 cm x 10.1 cm) green mottle

G   6 in x 6 in (15.2 cm x 15.2 cm) terra-cotta opaque (cut into random-size tesserae)

LIZARDS CACTUS POT

Approximate number of pieces   180 plus background tesserae

A   3 in x 5 in (7.6 cm x 12.7 cm) iridescent dark green and white wispy (cut into ½ in x ½ in or 1.3 cm x 1.3 cm tesserae)

B   2 in x 3 in (5 cm x 7.6 cm) red and white wispy (cut into ½ in x ½ in or 1.3 cm x 1.3 cm tesserae)

C   1 in x 3 in (2.5 cm x 7.6 cm) black

D   2 in x 2½ in (5 cm x 6.3 cm) orange and white wispy (cut into ½ in x ½ in or 1.3 cm x 1.3 cm tesserae)

E   2 in x 2 in (5 cm x 5 cm) green mottle

F   2 in x 2 in (5 cm x 5 cm) iridescent white

G   4 in x 6 in (10.1 cm x 15.2 cm) terra-cotta opaque (cut into random-size tesserae)

1 Construct this project by following the instructions given for Direct Method (pp26–8). Background fill uses the random method, p27.

2 Use water-resistant tile adhesive to apply the tesserae and a sanded, terra-cotta-tinted grout to finish the exterior.

3 When putting soil and vegetation directly into a terra-cotta pot, select one that has been glazed on the interior. If one is not available, apply a water-resistant silicone sealant to the inside or plant the cacti in a smaller plastic container to be inserted into the terra-cotta pot.

HELPFUL HINT   When smaller tesserae (¼ in x ¼ in or 0.6 cm x 0.6 cm) are required for a project, it is often easier to cut a larger size tessera into a few pieces of the smaller size. Use the glass mosaic cutters (nippers) or a glass cutter to divide a tessera in half and from there into smaller shapes and sizes. See p37.

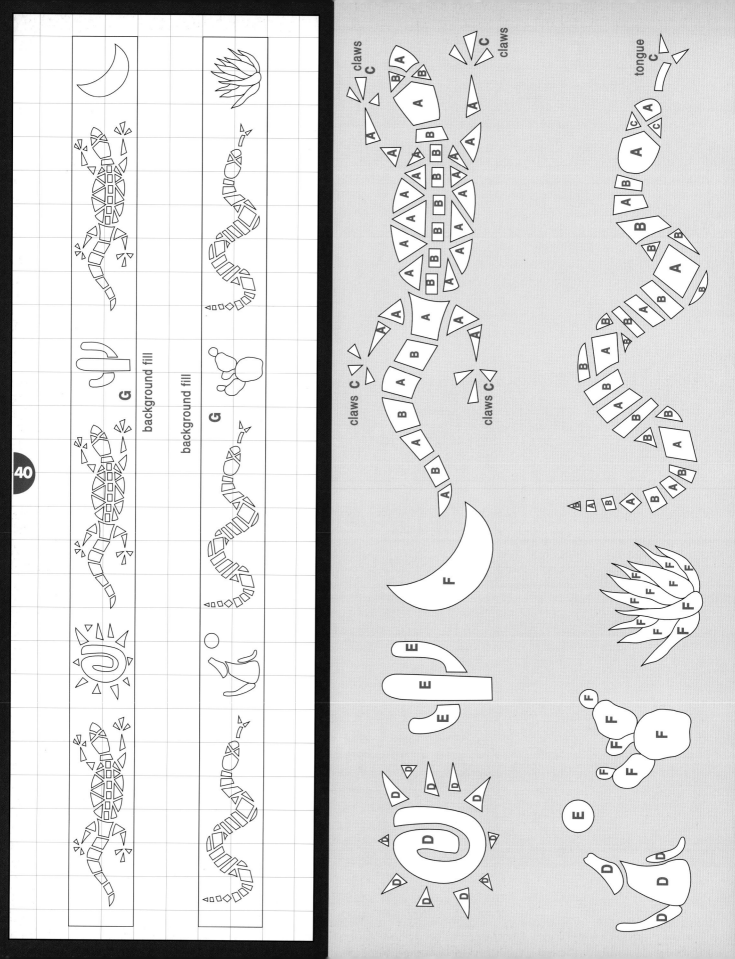

background fill

G

background fill

G

40

claws
C

C

claws

tongue
C

claws C

claws C

A

B

B

A

A

B

B

B

B

B

F

E

E

E

E

F

F

F

F

F

F

F

F

F

F

F

F

F

F

E

D

D

D

D

D

D

D

D

D

D

Old Tiles
terra-cotta pot

Plain terra-cotta pots can be fashioned into elegant containers with the addition of old or leftover ceramic tiles. Recycle your old pots and add a fresh look to your home or garden. If you have leftover scraps of stained glass, substitute them for the tiles. These will create charming pots unique to your setting.

CONTAINER   11 in (27.9 cm) high terra-cotta pot
APPROXIMATE NUMBER OF PIECES   64 plus background tesserae
TILES REQUIRED   Letters refer to the type of tiles used.
NOTE   The materials and instructions listed for this project are meant to be a guideline and are based on the size of terra-cotta container we purchased at our local home and garden center. Availability of sizes and shapes may vary, depending on where you live. Adjust the quantity and size of tiles to accommodate the pot you wish to decorate. To allow for matching colors and patterns you may need more tiles.

A   4—3 in x 3 in (7.6 cm x 7.6 cm) green glazed ceramic tiles
B   4—3 in x 3 in (7.6 cm x 7.6 cm) burgundy glazed ceramic tiles
C   12—3 in x 3 in (7.6 cm x 7.6 cm) white and patterned glazed ceramic tiles

1 Construct this project by following the instructions given for Direct Method (pp26–8). Background fill uses the random method, p27.
2 Use water-resistant tile adhesive to apply the tile pieces and a sanded, terra-cotta-tinted grout to finish the exterior.
3 When putting soil and vegetation directly into a terra-cotta pot, select one that has been glazed on the interior. If one is not available, apply a water-resistant silicone sealant to the inside or put your plant into a smaller plastic container to be inserted into the terra-cotta pot.

Special instructions
1 Measure 4½ in (11.4 cm) from the bottom and mark several points around the pot exterior. With a pencil, draw a line connecting these points to make a guideline around the circumference of the pot.
2 Use a measuring tape and mark 8 equally distanced points on the circumference line. These points will act as a gauge for positioning the green (A) and burgundy (B) tiles.
3 Cut the tiles (A and B) into 4 equal sections by scoring from one opposing corner to another and breaking into 4 triangular pieces. Score and break each of these pieces

in half, dividing each tile into 8 segments.
4 Cut the remaining tiles into random-size pieces no larger than approximately ½ in x ½ in (1.3 cm x 1.3 cm).
5 Adhere the green and burgundy tile pieces to the container, centering the tiles on the 8 points marked along the circumference line. Fill in the background with the random-size tile pieces (C).
6 Complete the project by following the instructions for *Applying the grout* and *Cleaning the finished piece* (p28), given in Direct Method.

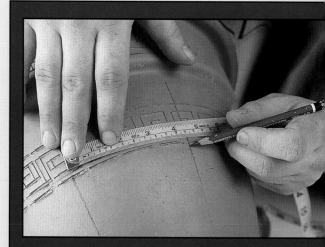

HELPFUL HINT Ceramic tiles can be cut with either a glass cutter or a tile cutter. Use an inexpensive disposable steel-wheel glass cutter when cutting the tiles for this project.

Lily Pond birdbath

Turn your yard into a garden of earthly delights with
the installation of this exquisite birdbath. Songbirds
frolicking and splashing in the water-filled basin will
be a scene your friends and family will enjoy.

SUPPORT STRUCTURE   precast concrete birdbath—24 in (60.9 cm) high with 18½ in (46.9 cm) diameter basin
APPROXIMATE NUMBER OF PIECES   112 plus background tesserae
GLASS REQUIRED   Letters refer to the type of glass used on pattern pieces (p46).
NOTE   The materials and instructions listed for this project are meant to be a guideline and are based on the size and style of precast concrete birdbath we purchased at our local garden center. Availability of sizes and shapes may vary, depending on where you live. Adjust the quantity and size of glass pieces to accommodate the birdbath you wish to decorate. To allow for matching colors and patterns you may have to purchase more glass.

A   12 in x 12 in (30.5 cm x 30.5 cm) pink and white opaque
B   1 in x 3 in (2.5 cm x 7.6 cm) yellow and white wispy (cut into small pieces of random-size tesserae)
C   12 in x 12 in (30.5 cm x 30.5 cm) dark green and white wispy
D   12 in x 12 in (30.5 cm x 30.5 cm) light blue and white opaque (cut into random-size tesserae)
E   12 in x 18 in (30.5 cm x 45.7 cm) iridescent blue and white opaque (cut 100—1 in x ½ in or 2.5 cm x 1.3 cm tesserae; cut balance into random-size tesserae)
F   iridescent clear glass nuggets (medium)—optional

Special instructions

Select a birdbath made of concrete that has been fully cured and not treated with any type of sealant. Choose one that is simple in design and has a surface that is fairly regular. Make sure the structure is clean and free of grease and dust. Use a cement-based adhesive that has high bond strength and water resistance to apply the glass pieces to the birdbath (we used ceramic tile thin-set mortar). Once the mortar has cured, it should not be affected by prolonged exposure to extreme temperatures or water and frost. For added bond strength and water resistance, additives are available and can be mixed with the mortar. We used this same mortar to grout between the glass pieces. Using the mortar for adhering and grouting required a combination of the direct and indirect methods.

1 Follow the steps given for *Preparing the pattern* given for Indirect Method (p29). This birdbath has one large central water lily motif surrounded by 4 small water lilies and 8 lily pads. You will require additional copies of the small water lily pattern.

2 Follow the steps given for *Preparing the glass pieces* described in Direct Method (pp26–7).

3 Follow the instructions for *Placement of the glass pieces onto the vinyl* (p30). Arrange all the pieces for the water lilies onto the vinyl. The lily pads (C) and the random-size tesserae (D and E) will be applied directly to the mortar.

4 Prepare enough mortar to cover approximately a quarter to a half of the inside surface of the basin. Add the dry mortar mix to water, and mix to a thick, smooth, creamy consistency. Allow the mixture to sit and slake for approximately 10 minutes. For exact measurements of water, dry mortar mix, etc., read and follow the manufacturer's directions.

5 Decide where you would like to position the 4 small water lilies in the basin of the birdbath. With a small trowel or rubber spatula, spread a layer of mortar mix (approximately ¹⁄₁₆ in to ⅛ in or 0.15 cm to 0.3 cm thick) over these locations and in the center

where the large water lily motif is to be applied.

6 Apply the large and small water lilies to the mortar, using the instructions given in the Indirect Method—*Applying the glass mosaic* (p31). Remember not to remove the vinyl until the mortar has cured for at least 24 hours.

7 Taking care not to disturb the water lilies, apply the wet mortar mix to the remaining uncovered areas. Do not spread mortar on more area than can be covered with the tesserae in 15 minutes. Press the lily pad pieces (C) and the background tesserae (D and E) in place, as described in the Direct Method, pp27–8. Fit pieces as closely as possible in a random fashion without the pieces touching. Use the glass cutter or mosaic nippers to trim pieces if necessary. Cover the bottom and sides of the interior of the basin.

NOTE Because edges of the glass pieces may be sharp, do not allow pieces to protrude over the lip of the basin. Prepare additional mortar mix as required.

OPTIONAL For an added touch, set a few glass nuggets (F) into the basin to give the appearance of water bubbles.

8 Immediately, while the mortar is still fresh, use a water-dampened sponge to wipe the excess mortar off the face of the glass pieces.

9 Apply the 1 in x 1½ in (2.5 cm x 3.8 cm) tesserae pieces to the outer rim of the basin, as described in steps 7 and 8 above. Refer to the photograph for placement.

10 Allow the mortar to cure for 24 hours.

11 Follow the instructions for *Applying the grout* given for Direct Method (p28) to fill the crevices between the glass pieces. Use the same mortar mix to grout that was used to adhere the glass pieces to the birdbath. Allow to set for 24 hours.

12 Clean the finished surface of the birdbath by wiping with a damp sponge and then polishing with a dry cloth. A paint scraper or utility knife can be used to scrape away any grout on the glass pieces that will not buff off.

13 Allow the birdbath to fully cure for several days before filling with water.

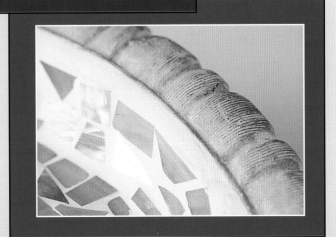

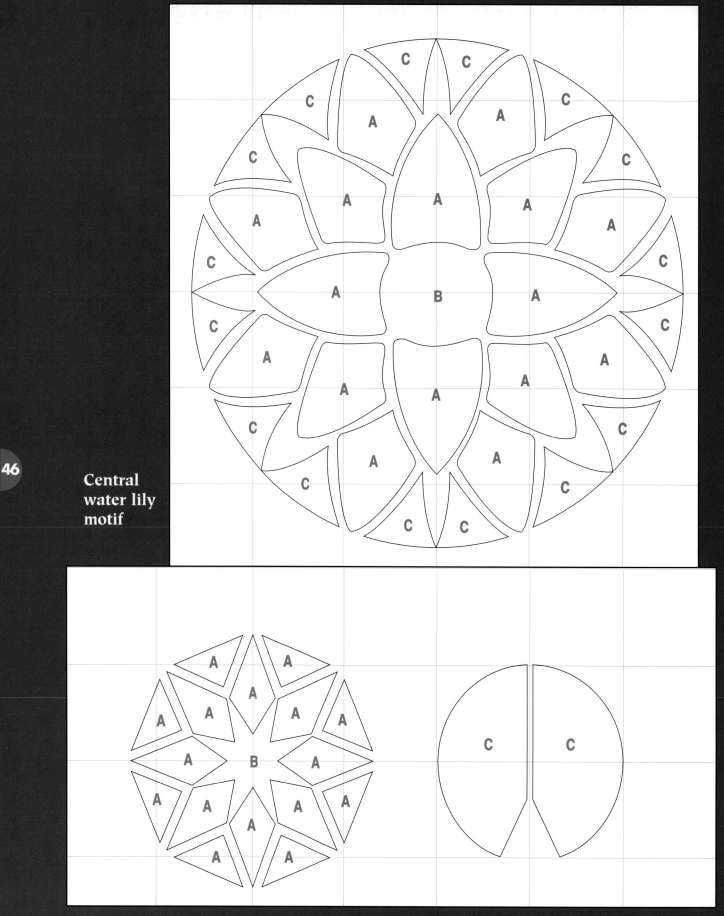

46

**Central
water lily
motif**

Small water lily motif

Leaf motif

Lotus & Dragonfly
wall hanging

Dragonflies flitting across a pond filled with fragrant lotus blossoms create a tranquil scene that is captured in this mosaic wall hanging. You will enjoy the reflections of light dancing off the mirrored glass that accent this exceptional piece.

MOSAIC PANEL SIZE   16 in x 16 in (40.6 cm x 40.6 cm)
TOTAL NUMBER OF PIECES   196 plus background and random tesserae
GLASS REQUIRED   Letters refer to the type of glass used on pattern pieces (p49).
This quantity of glass is the exact amount needed for the pattern. To allow for
matching textures and grain you may have to purchase more glass.

A   6 in x 12 in (15.2 cm x 30.5 cm) cranberry pink and white opal

B   8 in x 12 in (20.3 cm x 30.5 cm) emerald, spring green, and light green
ring mottle

C   1 in x 2 in (2.5 cm x 5 cm) yellow and white wispy

D   8 in x 12 in (20.3 cm x 30.5 cm) iridescent white (cut into small random-
size tesserae)

E   1 in x 2 in (2.5 cm x 5 cm) cobalt blue

F   3 in x 4 in (7.6 cm x 10.1 cm) iridescent clear texture

G   4 in x 6 in (10.1 cm x 15.2 cm) mirrored green semi-antique (cut 4—$^{15}/_{16}$
in x $^{15}/_{16}$ in or 2.3 cm x 2.3 cm and 12—$^{7}/_{16}$ in x $^{7}/_{16}$ in or 1.1 cm x 1.1 cm
tesserae; and the balance into small random-size tesserae)

H   5 in x 8 in (12.7 cm x 20.3 cm) cobalt blue and emerald green ring mottle
(cut 24—$^{15}/_{16}$ in x $^{15}/_{16}$ in or 2.3 cm x 2.3 cm and 32—$^{7}/_{16}$ in x $^{15}/_{16}$ in or 1.1 cm
x 2.3 cm tesserae)

J   5 in x 12 in (12.7 cm x 30.5 cm) mirrored blue semi-antique (cut 24—$^{15}/_{16}$
in x $^{15}/_{16}$ in or 2.3 cm x 2.3 cm and 20—$^{7}/_{16}$ in x $^{15}/_{16}$ in or 1.1 cm x 2.3 cm
tesserae; and the balance into small random-size tesserae)

NOTE   The letter I is not used in this listing.

48

1 Construct this project by following
the instructions given for Direct
Method (pp26–8).

2 Guidelines to construct the base
for this stained glass mosaic are given
in *Making wood base/support
structures–Trivet and wall hangings*
(pp32–3).

HELPFUL HINT Sheets of art
glass composed of two or more
colors mixed together can vary
greatly in shade from one part
of a sheet to another. The glass
pieces for the lotus flowers (A)
have all been cut from the
same sheet of cranberry pink
and white opal, and the leaves
and pods (B) are from one
sheet of mixed green ring
mottle. When cutting out the
required glass pieces, take
advantage of the effect created
by varying shades and tones.

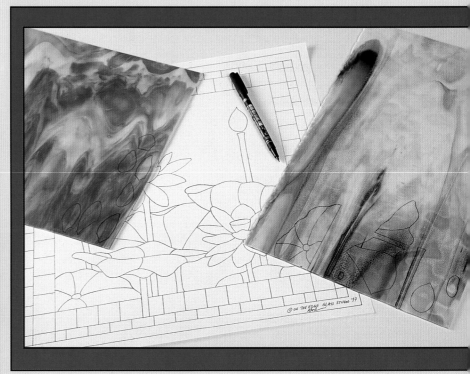

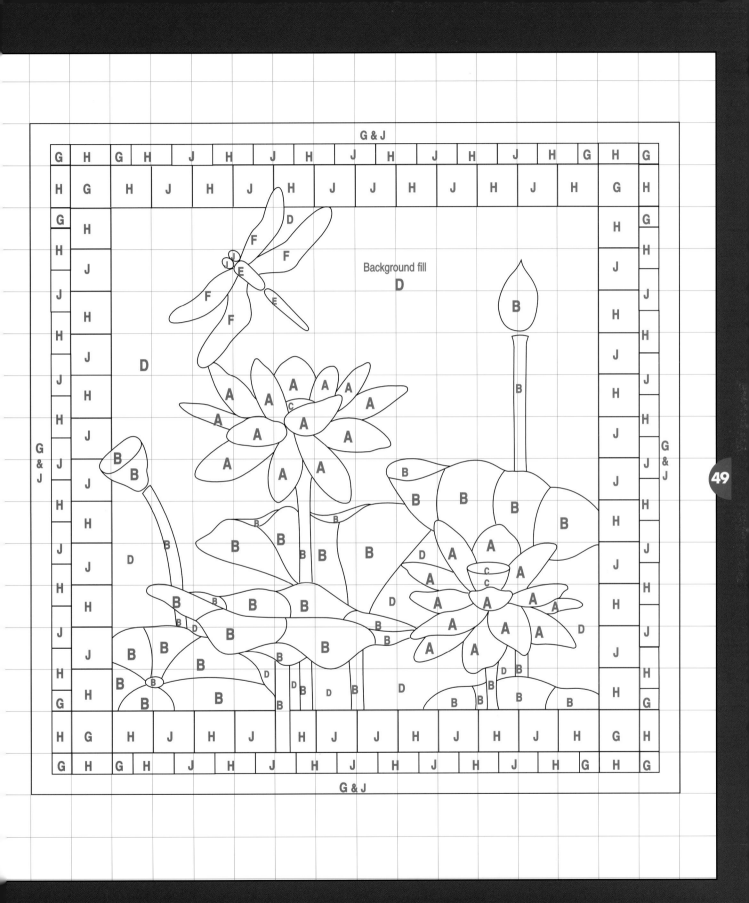

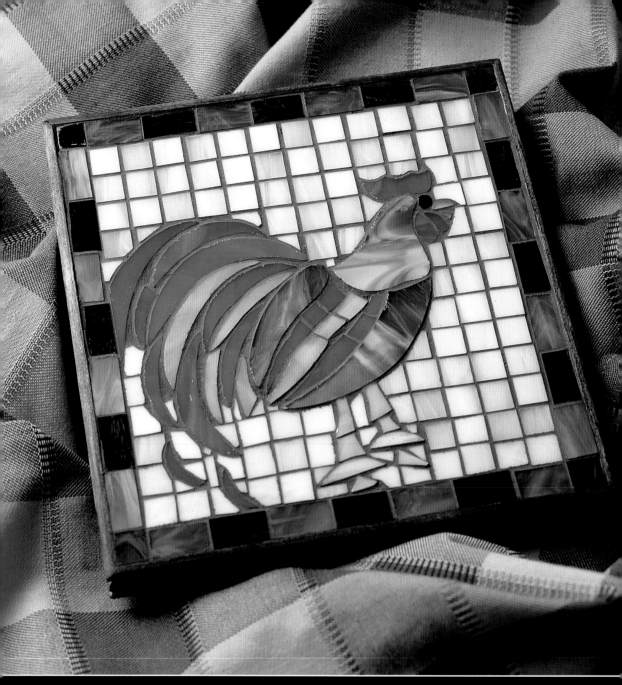

Cock-a-Doodle-Dude trivet

Every morning deserves to be started with a welcome from this feisty fellow. Whether hanging around on your kitchen wall or perched on the counter top, you'll have something to crow about when this rooster mosaic takes up residence in your kitchen.

A 2 in x 4 in (5 cm x 10.1 cm) iridescent dark green and white wispy (cut 12—$^{15}/_{16}$ in x $^{7}/_{16}$ in or 2.3 cm x 1.1 cm and 4—$^{7}/_{16}$ in x $^{7}/_{16}$ in or 1.1 cm x 1.1 cm tesserae)

B 2 in x 4 in (5 cm x 10.1 cm) dark amber and white wispy (cut 16—$^{15}/_{16}$ in x $^{7}/_{16}$ in or 2.3 cm x 1.1 cm tesserae)

C 1 in x 2 in (2.5 cm x 5 cm) orange opaque

D 2 in x 2 in (5 cm x 5 cm) orange and white streaky opaque

E 3½ in x 3½ in (8.9 cm x 8.9 cm) amber and white opaque

F 4 in x 5 in (10.1 cm x 12.7 cm) red and white wispy

G 2 in x 3 in (5 cm x 7.6 cm) pale green and amber wispy

H 1 in x 1 in (2.5 cm x 2.5 cm) iridescent black

J 1 in x 1 in (2.5 cm x 2.5 cm) yellow opaque

K 5 in x 5 in (12.7 cm x 12.7 cm) white wispy (cut into ½ in x ½ in or 1.3 cm x 1.3 cm tesserae)

L 2 in x 2 in (5 cm x 5 cm) iridescent white (cut into ½ in x ½ in or 1.3 cm x 1.3 cm tesserae)

NOTE The letter I was not used in this listing.

1 Construct this project by following the instructions given for Direct Method (pp26–8).
2 Guidelines to construct the base for this stained glass mosaic are given in *Making wood base/support structures—Trivet and wall hangings* (pp32–3).
NOTE The background of this mosaic project is filled in using the *opus tesselatum* method, p27.

HELPFUL HINT Randomly place the iridescent white tesserae (L) amongst the white pieces (K) to add a little interest to the background of this playful mosaic project.

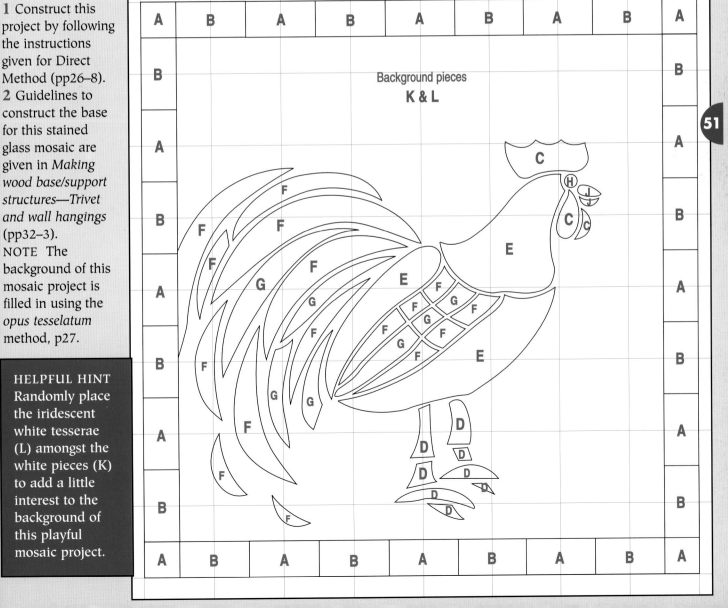

Background pieces
K & L

Sunflower wall hanging

The cheerful sunflower continues to be an inspiration to artists everywhere. Large golden blooms atop majestic stalks have a great presence in the garden and this sunny motif brightens our pretty wall hanging.

MOSAIC PANEL SIZE 16 in x 16 in (40.6 cm x 40.6 cm)
TOTAL NUMBER OF PIECES 240 plus background tesserae
GLASS REQUIRED Letters refer to the type of glass used on pattern pieces.
The quantity of glass is the exact amount needed for the pattern. To allow
for matching textures and grain you may have to purchase more glass.

A 8 in x 12 in (20.3 cm x 30.5 cm) yellow and white wispy

B 4 in x 7 in (10.1 cm x 17.8 cm) green and white ring mottle

C 2 in x 4 in (5 cm x 10.1 cm) green, brown, and white streaky

D 2 in x 4 in (5 cm x 10.1 cm) red and amber opal (cut into ¼ in x ¼ in or 0.6 cm x 0.6 cm tesserae)

E 3 in x 3 in (7.6 cm x 7.6 cm) green and orange ring mottle

F 2 in x 2 in (5 cm x 5 cm) medium amber and white wispy

G 3 in x 4 in (7.6 cm x 10.1 cm) mirrored amber semi-antique

H 6 in x 12 in (15.2 cm x 30.5 cm) iridescent purple cathedral (cut corner pieces plus 48—$^{15}/_{16}$ in x $^{15}/_{16}$ in or 2.3 cm x 2.3 cm tesserae)

J 4 in x 12 in (10.1 cm x 30.5 cm) dark blue and white wispy (cut into $^{15}/_{16}$ in x $^{15}/_{16}$ in or 2.3 cm x 2.3 cm tesserae)

K 4 in x 6 in (10.1 cm x 15.2 cm) pale blue and medium blue ring mottle

L 2 in x 3 in (5 cm x 7.6 cm) iridescent white (cut into ½ in x ½ in or 1.3 cm x 1.3 cm tesserae)

M 4 red glass nuggets (medium)

N 8 in x 12 in (20.3 cm x 30.5 cm) blue-gray and white ring mottle (cut into small random-size tesserae)

NOTE The letter I is not used in this listing.

1 Construct this project by following the instructions given for Direct Method (pp26–8).

2 Guidelines to construct the base for this stained glass mosaic are given in *Making wood base/support structures—Trivet and wall hangings* (pp32–3).

HELPFUL HINT
To create a soft muted backdrop that makes the sunflowers stand out, surround them with small tesserae randomly sized and positioned. *See p27.*

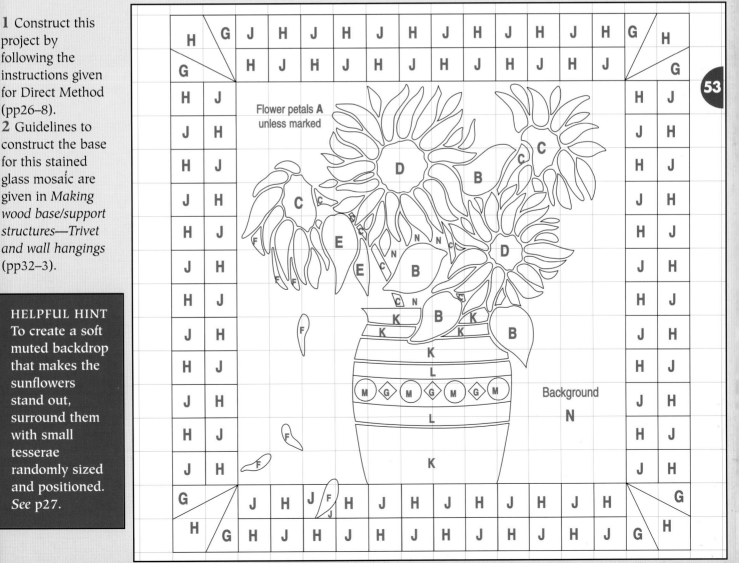

53

Relativity wall hanging and trivet

Bold colors and geometric shapes and lines give
this glass mosaic a dramatic flare. The addition
of faceted jewels and glass nuggets catch the
light to fill a room with gorgeous colors.

WALL HANGING

A   12 in x 12 in (30.5 cm x 30.5 cm) lilac and white opaque (cut into ½ in x ½ in or 1.3 cm x 1.3 cm tesserae)

B   4 in x 5 in (10.1 cm x 12.7 cm) poppy red opal (cut 1—1 in x 1½ in or 2.5 cm x 3.8 cm and the balance into ½ in x ½ in or 1.3 cm x 1.3 cm tesserae)

C   3½ in x 7 in (8.9 cm x 17.8 cm) steel blue opal

D   2 in x 5½ in (5 cm x 13.9 cm) dusty lilac opal

E   3 in x 3 in (7.6 cm x 7.6 cm) emerald green opal

F   3 in x 10 in (7.6 cm x 25.4 cm) iridescent dark blue and white wispy

G   12 in x 12 in (30.5 cm x 30.5 cm) iridescent lilac and white wispy (cut the larger pattern shape first; then cut the balance into ½ in x ½ in or 1.3 cm x 1.3 cm tesserae)

H   38mm x 28mm blue rectangular faceted jewel

I   20mm x 45mm red oval faceted jewel

J   14mm x 60mm amethyst oval faceted jewel

K   35mm amethyst round faceted jewel

L   35mm green round faceted jewel

M   30mm blue round faceted jewel

N   24mm red round faceted jewel

P   24mm rose round faceted jewel

Q   iridescent lilac glass nugget (medium)

R   iridescent blue glass nugget (medium)

S   iridescent red glass nugget (medium)

NOTE   The letter O has not been used in this listing.

1 Construct this project by following the instructions given for Direct Method (pp26–8).

2 Guidelines to construct the base for this stained glass mosaic are given in *Making wood base/support structures—Trivet and wall hangings* (pp32–3).

NOTE   The lilac and white opaque background tesserae (A) were applied using the *opus tesselatum* technique (p27). By changing the direction of the sections of iridescent lilac and white tesserae (G), interest and movement are created within this geometric design.

TRIVET

A   5 in x 8 in (12.7 cm x 20.3 cm) lilac and white opaque (cut into ½ in x ½ in or 1.3 cm x 1.3 cm tesserae)

B   2 in x 3 in (5 cm x 7.6 cm) poppy red opal

C   4 in x 5 in (10.1 cm x 12.7 cm) steel blue opal

D   1 in x 2 in (2.5 cm x 5 cm) dusty lilac opal

E   2 in x 2 in (5 cm x 5 cm) emerald green opal

F   2 in x 3 in (5 cm x 7.6 cm) iridescent dark blue and white wispy

G   3 in x 6 in (7.6 cm x 15.2 cm) iridescent lilac and white wispy (cut ½ in x ½ in or 1.3 cm x 1.3 cm tesserae)

The direction of glass is changed to give this unusual effect.

HELPFUL HINTS

A. Place a few iridescent lilac and white tesserae (G) at random amongst the lilac and white opaque pieces (A) to add interest to the background of the mosaic.

B. Add depth to the mosaic by turning over some of the opal glass pieces and applying them to the base piece with the reverse side up. The underside of these glass sheets is slightly textured and contains slight variations in color that are a nice diversion from the smoother and more even toned topside.

Special instructions

Choose a section from the main design to make a smaller wall hanging or trivet to complement this mosaic piece. The photograph shows the design elements of the top left corner of the wall hanging used to create the smaller piece.

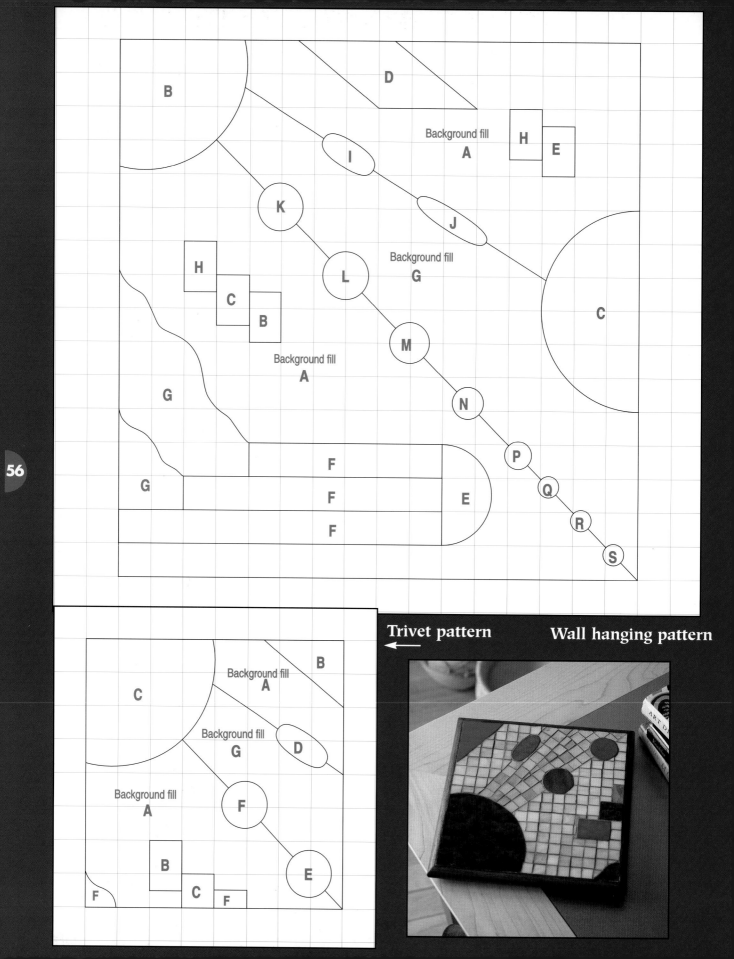

Trivet pattern

Wall hanging pattern

Distraction wall hanging and trivet

The contrasting colors and divergent lines of these mosaic pieces offer a distraction to the mind's eye. Place the wall hanging where it can reflect the light and enjoy the play of colors

WALL HANGING	TRIVET
MOSAIC PANEL SIZE 16 in x 16 in (40.6 cm x 40.6 cm)	8 in x 8 in (20.3 cm x 20.3 cm)
TOTAL NUMBER OF PIECES 14 plus tesserae	4 plus tesserae

GLASS REQUIRED   Letters refer to the type of glass used on the pattern (p59).
The quantity of glass listed for the wall hanging and the trivet is the exact amount needed for the patterns.
To allow for matching textures and grain you may have to purchase more glass.

WALL HANGING

A   4 in x 9 in (10.1 cm x 22.8 cm) mirrored purple semi-antique
B   3 in x 9 in (7.6 cm x 22.8 cm) red and white wispy
C   6 in x 10 in (15.2 cm x 25.4 cm) steel blue opal
D   9 in x 15 in (22.8 cm x 38.1 cm) lime green and white streaky
E   12 in x 16 in (30.5 cm x 40.6 cm) white (cut into small random-size tesserae)

TRIVET

A   1 in x 1 in (2.5 cm x 2.5 cm) mirrored purple semi-antique
B   1 in x 1 in (2.5 cm x 2.5 cm) red and white wispy
C   6 in x 6 in (15.2 cm x 15.2 cm) steel blue opal
D   5 in x 12 in (12.7 cm x 30.5 cm) lime green and white streaky
E   4 in x 8 in (10.1 cm x 20.3 cm) white (cut into small random-size tesserae)

1 Construct this project by following the instructions given for Direct Method (pp26–8).
2 Guidelines to construct the base for this stained glass mosaic are given in *Making wood base/support structures—Trivet and wall hangings* (pp32–3).
NOTE The white background tesserae (A) were applied using the random method (p27). By using black grout in contrast to the white tesserae, this abstract mosaic design becomes even more distinctive.

58

HELPFUL HINTS
A. Create an element of tension in the section containing lime green and white wispy glass (D) by breaking the glass into large angular pieces.
B. Turn over the steel blue opal piece (C), in the shape of a partial circle, so that the underside is face up to give more visual depth.

The large lime green shapes on the pattern can be cut into smaller pieces, if desired.

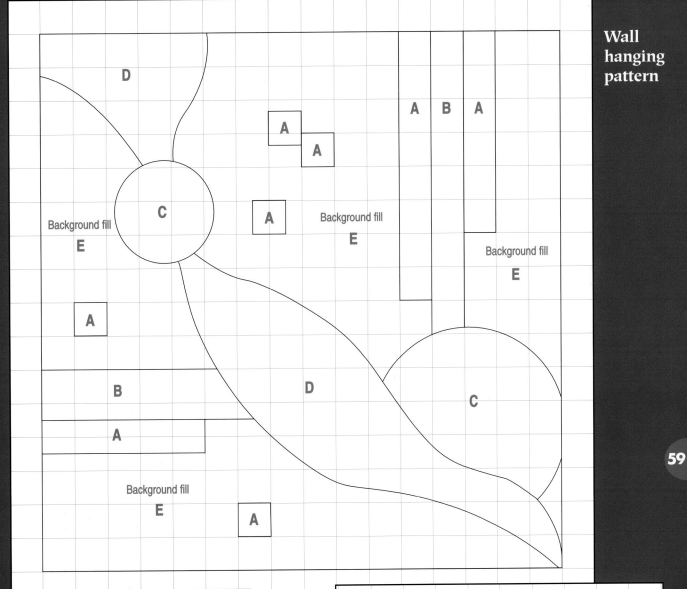

D

A

B A

A B A

A

C

Background fill

E

Background fill

E

Background fill

E

A

B

A

D

C

Background fill

E

A

Trivet pattern →

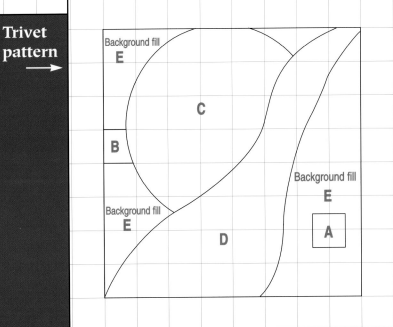

Background fill

E

C

B

Background fill

E

Background fill

E

D

A

Stained Glass
Mosaic tabletop

A variety of methods can be used to make a glass mosaic top for interior use. You can secure a plywood sheet (cut to size) to an existing table base and frame it with wood trim molding, and then apply a glass mosaic using either of the two basic mosaic techniques. Tables with wooden surfaces have the mosaic applied directly. The surface should be prepared by removing any lacquers, paints, or sealants and abrading with sandpaper.

To design a glass mosaic table top you can convert one of the patterns in this book to the appropriate size. Or you can adapt the main design elements from the patterns on upholstered chairs and furniture in the room where the table will stand. This is particularly effective for dining room and kitchen tables. All that is needed is a fabric swatch, tracing paper, and a pencil. Lay the swatch on a flat work surface and place a sheet of tracing paper on the material. Trace the pattern outlines onto the paper with a pencil. Determine the size of mosaic required and draw the outline onto a sheet of pattern paper. Decide which design elements you would like to develop into the mosaic and transfer to the pattern paper, using any of the methods described in Basic Techniques, *Copying patterns* (p13). Choose a selection of glass that will complement the upholstery and other features in the room. Once you have determined which mosaic technique you will use, start assembling the mosaic. Once completed, you will have a beautiful and unique piece of furniture.

Trace the pattern onto vellum. Using carbon paper transfer the design to the tabletop base/support structure.

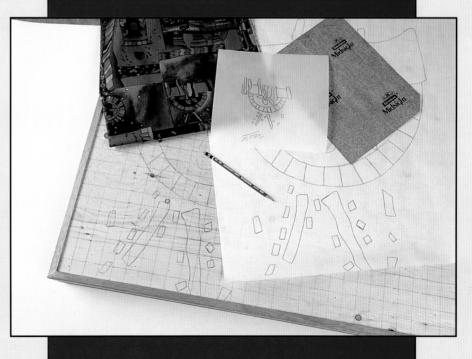

Fish Faerie backsplash

This whimsical creature is the perfect backdrop for bathroom or kitchen, or any area where water is used. In this example, the shell-shaped background is fashioned after the mirror image of the pedestal basin. However, the shell background blends with any decor and can be a focal point for your decorating scheme

BACKSPLASH DIMENSIONS 17¼ in high x 20 in wide (43.8 cm x 50 cm)
TOTAL NUMBER OF PIECES 67 plus tesserae
GLASS REQUIRED Letters refer to the type of glass used on pattern pieces (p64).
The quantity of glass is the exact amount needed for the pattern. To allow for matching textures and grain you may have to purchase more glass.

A 6 in x 10 in (15.2 cm x 25.4 cm) iridescent black (with fish scale pattern)

B 5 in x 15 in (12.7 cm x 38.1 cm) iridescent clear reeded texture

C 2 in x 4 in (5 cm x 10.1 cm) iridescent clear heavy texture

D 4 in x 10 in (10.1 cm x 25.4 cm) iridescent peach and white wispy (cut 2 pieces for bottom corners of clam shell; cut 24—½ in x ⅝ in or 1.3 cm x 1.5 cm tesserae; cut balance into ¼ in x ¼ in or 0.6 cm x 0.6 cm tesserae)

E 2 in x 4 in (5 cm x 10.1 cm) mirrored amber semi-antique

F 1 in x 7 in (2.5 cm x 17.7 cm) 3mm mirror

G 18 in x 18 in (45.7 cm x 45.7 cm) iridescent white (cut 112—½ in x ⅝ in or 1.3 cm x 1.5 cm tesserae; cut balance into ½ in x ½ in or 1.3 cm x 1.3 cm tesserae)

H 4 in x 10 in (10.1 cm x 25.4 cm) teal green and white wispy

J 1 iridescent black glass nugget (medium)

K 1 iridescent white glass nugget (medium)

L 1 iridescent teal green glass nugget (medium)

M 1 in x 1 in (2.5 cm x 2.5 cm) red opaque

N 1 in x 1 in (2.5 cm x 2.5 cm) mirrored green semi-antique

NOTE The letter I was not used in this listing.

1 Construct this project by following the instructions given for Direct Method (pp26–8).

Special instructions

The glass mosaic backsplash is assembled on a ½ in (1.3 cm) plywood base/support structure using the Direct Method. Once constructed, the mosaic is then fastened in place with screws. Here's how to do it.

Making the base/support structure

1 Trace the perimeter of the pattern outline onto an 18 in x 22 in (45.7 cm x 55.8 cm) piece of ½ in (1.3 cm) thick plywood. Align the straight bottom edge of the pattern with one edge of the plywood, to make maximum use of the material.

2 Cut along the traced outline with a jigsaw and remove the base from the main piece of plywood.

3 Remove any rough edges on the base piece with sandpaper.

4 Use the pattern as a guide to mark and then drill 4 holes in the base piece. Countersink the holes so that when the finished backsplash is fastened to the wall, the screw heads will not be raised above the plywood surface and interfere with the application of the covering glass pieces.

5 Trace all design lines from the pattern copy onto the base/support structure. Score the wood surface with a utility knife to give better adhesion.

Constructing the glass mosaic

Fabricate the mosaic by following the guidelines given for Direct Method (pp26–8).

1 Leave ¹⁄₁₆ in (0.15 cm) space between the edge of the glass and the edge of the base support structure when placing glass pieces. A border row of tesserae will be applied along the exposed wood edge so glass pieces cannot protrude.

2 Use a water-resistant tile adhesive and grout to prevent moisture damage.

3 Leave enough space around the screw holes so that when the mosaic is installed the screws can be tightened without damaging the surrounding tesserae.

4 Begin by applying the glass pieces for the faerie. We have cut the pieces for her hair with a glass bandsaw. If you do not have access to a bandsaw, cut tesserae pieces and use the outline of the hair design lines as a guide for placement.

5 Place the tesserae pieces for arms, neck, and shoulders in rows, following the curvature of the lines. Lay the eyes, nose, mouth, and eyebrow pieces first for the face. The eyebrows and nose are composed of fragments of the black iridescent glass (A). Complete by filling in with the tesserae (D), following the outline of the face and working inward. The body of the fish and the faerie's belt are filled in with small mirrored tesserae (colors as indicated on the pattern). The shaft of the scepter can be cut as two pieces of mirror or can be broken up into smaller tesserae. When adhering the wings to the base piece, be sure to cover the underside of the glass completely with the adhesive so that the plywood is not visible through the glass.

6 Attach the glass pieces for the background shell by applying the two bottom corner pieces (D) first. Continue by adhering a perimeter row of iridescent white tesserae (G) along the outline of the shell and on either side of the design lines to the left and right of the faerie. Use these lines as a guideline for the directional flow of the tesserae. See the photograph of the finished mosaic for placement of background fill which uses a combination of *opus tesselatum* and *opus vermiculatum* methods, p27.

7 Cover the exposed outer edge of the base/support structure with a row of tesserae (D and G). Place the correct color of border tesserae adjacent to the corresponding tesserae on the front of the mosaic. Do not allow any of the tesserae to protrude over the underside of the plywood base because this may interfere with installing the mosaic to the wall.

8 Allow the adhesive to cure for 24 hours. Grout (p28) and clean the project, taking care to leave the 4 screw holes open. Use a silicone grout sealant if moisture damage may be a concern.

Mounting the backsplash
1 Fit the mosaic against the wall in the desired location. Mark each point where the backsplash is to be fastened by inserting a pencil into the screw holes in the base and marking the wall behind. Remove the backsplash, drill the holes, and insert the appropriate plug or anchor.

2 Fasten the backsplash to the wall, using No.8 screws approximately 1½ in (3.8 cm) in length.

3 Butter (p27) the underside of several tesserae (G) and press into place over the heads of the screws. Once the adhesive has cured, grout and clean the four areas. If required, place a bead of silicone caulking along the bottom edge of the mosaic and the counter top or sink below.

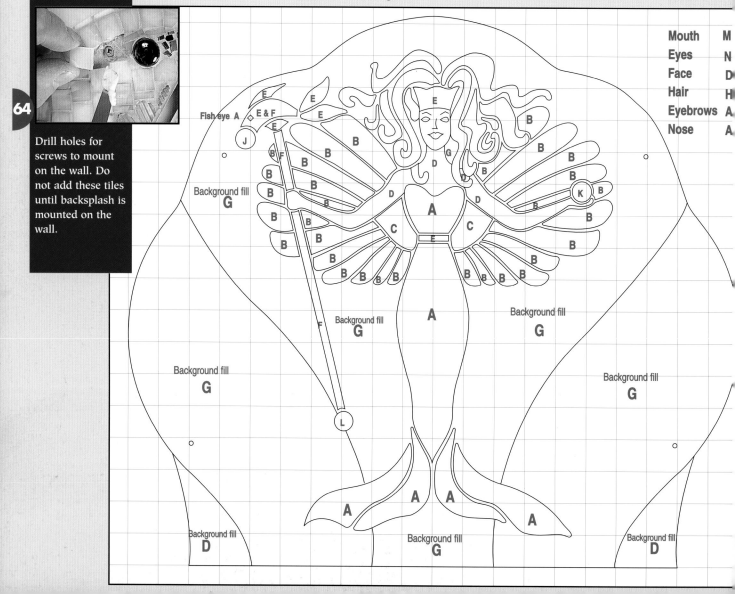

Drill holes for screws to mount on the wall. Do not add these tiles until backsplash is mounted on the wall.

Mouth	M
Eyes	N
Face	D
Hair	H
Eyebrows	A
Nose	A

64

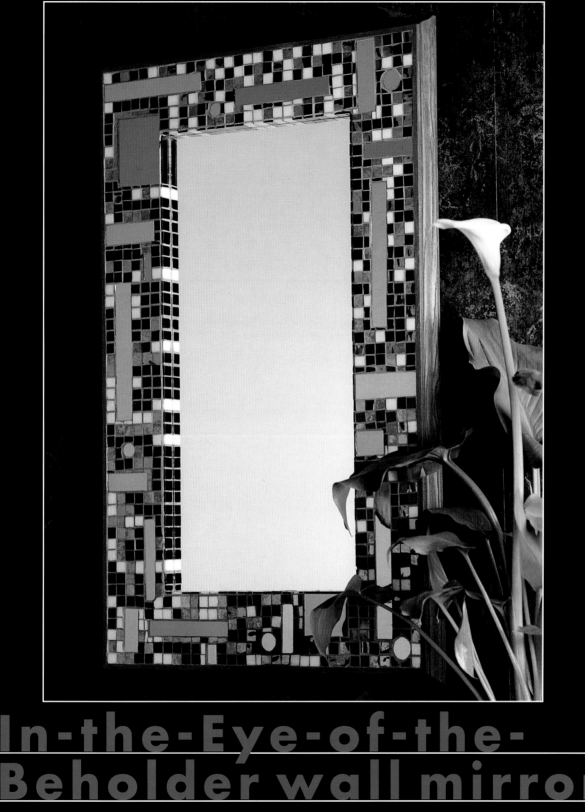

In-the-Eye-of-the-Beholder wall mirror

This glittering mosaic mirror is a striking accent for an entrance hall or living or dining room. It has a contemporary look and the mirrored glass mosaic pieces reflect muted color to give a room a special glow.

OUTSIDE DIMENSIONS OF MOSAIC   18 in x 30 in (45.7 cm x 76.2 cm)
TOTAL NUMBER OF PIECES   25 plus background tesserae
GLASS REQUIRED   Letters refer to the type of glass used on pattern pieces (p67). The quantity of glass is the exact amount needed for the pattern. To allow for matching textures and grain you may have to purchase more glass.

A   8 in x 8 in (20.3 cm x 20.3 cm) mirrored purple semi-antique
B   8 in x 8 in (20.3 cm x 20.3 cm) mirrored blue semi-antique
C   8 in x 8 in (20.3 cm x 20.3 cm) mirrored amber semi-antique
D   10 in x 12 in (25.4 cm x 30.5 cm) black (cut 8 in x 12 in or 20.3 cm x 30.5 cm portion into ½ in x ½ in or 1.3 cm x 1.3 cm background tesserae; cut 2 in x 12 in or 5 cm x 30.5 cm portion into ½ in x ⅝ in or 1.3 cm x 1.5 cm tesserae)
E   10 in x 12 in (25.4 cm x 30.5 cm) white (cut 8 in x 12 in or 20.3 cm x 30.5 cm portion into ½ in x ½ in or 1.3 cm x 1.3 cm background tesserae; cut 2 in x 12 in or 5 cm x 30.5 cm portion into ½ in x ⅝ in or 1.3 cm x 1.5 cm tesserae)
F   10 in x 12 in (25.4 cm x 30.5 cm) iridescent black (cut 8 in x 12 in or 20.3 cm x 30.5 cm portion into ½ in x ½ in or 1.3 cm x 1.3 cm background tesserae; cut 2 in x 12 in or 5 cm x 30.5 cm portion into ½ in x ⅝ in or 1.3 cm x 1.5 cm tesserae)
G   12 in x 24 in (30.5 cm x 60.9 cm) 3mm mirror

1 Construct this project by following the instructions given for Direct Method (pp26–8).
2 Guidelines to construct the support structure are given in *Making wood base/support structures—Wall mirror* (pp33–4).

Special instructions
1 Transfer the pattern to the 3½ in (8.9 cm) wide framework upon which the mosaic is to be applied. Then measure the recessed area where the 3mm mirror will be placed. The opening will be approximately 11 in x 23 in (27.9 cm x 58.4 cm).
2 Cut the 3mm mirror ⅛ in (0.3 cm) less in height and width for ease of placement into the opening and to allow for slight deviations in the frame size. For example, if the opening is 11 in x 23 in (27.9 cm x 58.4 cm), the mirror size will be 10⅞ in x 22⅞ in (27.6 cm x 58.1 cm).
3 Adhere the mirror to the plywood base with a neutral curing silicone. This adhesive is noncorrosive and will not affect the silver backing of the mirror.

Allow to cure (see the manufacturer's instructions and follow any safety precautions listed).
4 Cover the mirror surface with masking tape. Leave an allowance of approximately ¼ in (0.6 cm) free of tape, around the perimeter of the mirror.

5 Apply the glass pieces and tesserae to the framework using the Direct Method of mosaic construction. The ½ in x ½ in (1.3 cm x 1.3 cm) tesserae pieces (D, E, F) are placed in random color order. Do not allow any pieces to overhang the recessed opening where the mirror is now located.

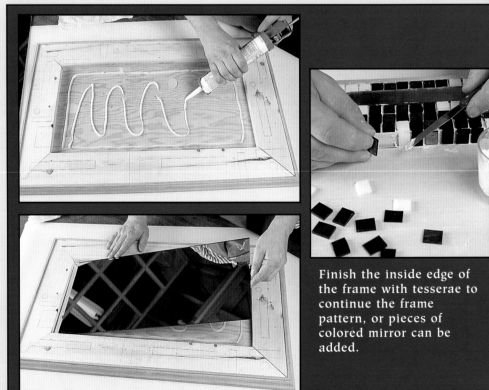

Finish the inside edge of the frame with tesserae to continue the frame pattern, or pieces of colored mirror can be added.

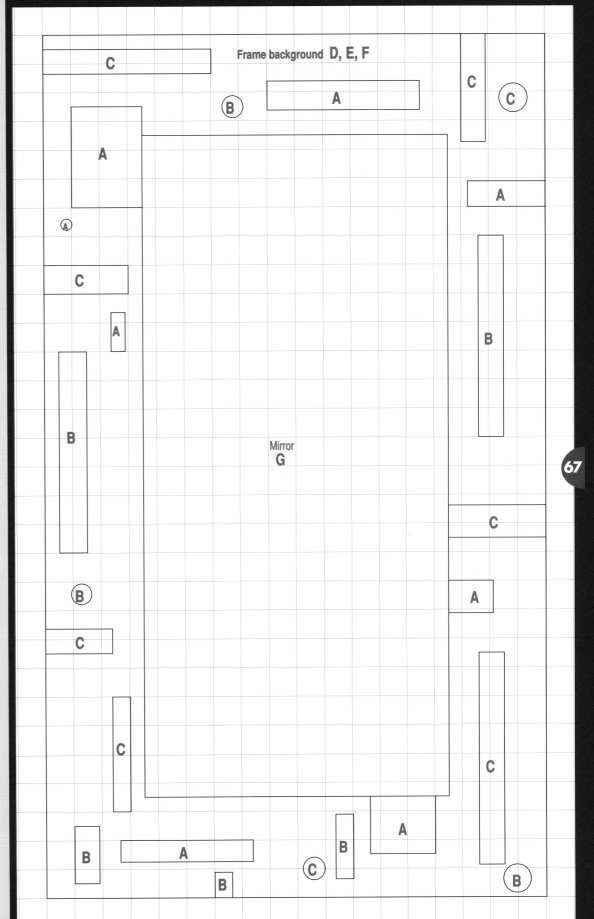

6 Cover the exposed wood edges between the mirror and the mosaic framework by adhering the ½ in x ⅝ in (1.3 cm x 1.5 cm) tesserae pieces (D, E, F) to the wood with the tile adhesive. Pieces of colored mirror can be substituted in those areas adjacent to the larger mirrored pieces in the mosaic framework.

7 Allow to cure, then complete the project by following the directions given for *Applying the grout* and *Cleaning the finished piece* (p28).

8 Remove the masking tape covering the mirror piece.

9 Hang the mirror lengthwise or sideways. See *Mounting wall hangings and mirrors* (p34).

Stained Glass Mosaic Garden Stones

A garden is one of the great pleasures of life. Whether large or small it can be a perfect retreat for quiet hours, a relaxing place to entertain family and friends, or a growing wonderland of flowers and shrubs that expresses your creative design. Give your garden special focus with beautiful glass mosaic garden stones that you have crafted yourself. Use them for pathways, to surround a fish pond, to accent a flower bed, to brighten a shady corner, or to make a striking patio. Watching the play of light on the many pieces of sparkling glass in your garden stones will bring hours of enjoyment and make your yard the envy of the neighborhood.

Construction Techniques

Materials

3 copies of pattern
Clear adhesive-backed vinyl
Masking tape
Glass pieces for project
Newspaper
Dish soap and water
Petroleum jelly
Plywood board
Galvanized hardware cloth (wire
  mesh)
Ready-mixed mortar cement
Water
Tint (optional)
Sand

Tools

Apron
Safety glasses
Utility knife or scissors
Mold/Form
Permanent waterproof fine-tipped
  marker
Cork-backed straightedge
Glass cutter
Glass mosaic nippers (optional)
Running pliers
Breaking/grozing pliers
Carborundum stone or glass grinder
Small containers or jars
Soft cloths
Tweezers
Wire cutters
Rubber or latex gloves
Respirator or dust mask
Plastic watertight mixing container
Trowel or wooden straightedge
Plastic sheet
Spray bottle
Screwdriver
Sponge
Soft bristled brushes and/or
  toothbrush
Razor blades and/or paint scraper
Dental picks (optional)
Small garden spade or shovel

Choosing a form/mold   Garden stone projects are made using the indirect (reverse) method (p29) which requires a form or mold that is filled with cement that hardens into concrete. This is the support structure that holds the mosaic in place. There are many commercial molds available in round, square, rectangular, and hexagonal shapes as well as heart, butterfly, or curved sectional molds to use as borders. Many of the patterns in this book have been designed for these molds. As well, you can use plastic food storage containers and baking pans that you may have around the house (do not reuse for food).

NOTE   The sides of the mold must be perpendicular (straight up and down) or at an outward angle to the bottom of the form. Inward angled sides will prevent removal of the garden stone without damaging it or breaking the mold.

Selecting the glass   Choose the correct glass for the glass mosaic.

1 For the best results, the surface of the glass should be as smooth and flat as possible.

2 If you use textured glass, place the glass so that the smooth side faces down onto the clear adhesive-backed vinyl. See *Placing the glass pieces* (p72). If the textured side of the glass is pressed face down onto the vinyl, the glass pieces may become partially or completely buried when the wet cement mixture is poured. The air pockets between the textures in the glass and the vinyl create space into which cement can ooze and this will often lift the glass from the vinyl.

3 Choose colorful and contrasting opaque glasses for their surface reflective qualities. Keep the choice of translucent glasses to a minimum because they may appear dull and discolored when surrounded by concrete. Iridescent glasses add a shimmer to the garden stones and are an exciting accent to most patterns.

Preparing the pattern
An accurate pattern is an essential step in making a garden stone. Follow these guidelines:

1 Make 3 copies (p13) of the pattern you have chosen. There should be a space or line thickness of at least $^1/_{16}$ in (0.15 cm) between each glass piece.

2 Use one pattern copy as a guide for cutting and breaking glass pieces to the correct size and shape. Use the second copy to cut out any pattern piece for which a template is required (when cutting opaque glass), remembering to cut inside the pattern lines. Use the third copy to place beneath the clear adhesive-backed vinyl to act as a guide for laying out the glass pieces for the garden stone.

3 Verify that the pattern fits within the form by trimming all excess paper away from the outline of the third pattern copy and placing it inside the form. The pattern must lie flat on the bottom of the form. These garden stone patterns have been designed to allow approximately $^1/_2$ in (1.3 cm) space between the interior walls of the form and the outer edge of the glass pieces. If you have to make adjustments to the pattern to ensure a better fit, be sure to adjust the other 2 copies as well.

4 Remove the pattern from the form. On a light table, place the pattern copy face down and trace the design lines onto the reverse side. If a light table is not available, tape the pattern onto a window (with the

design facing outside), and trace.

5 Tape the pattern copy to a flat work surface or board, with the reverse side facing upward.

6 Cut a piece of clear, adhesive-backed vinyl, approximately ½ in (1.3 cm) larger than the pattern. Peel the paper backing from the vinyl. Position the vinyl over the pattern taped to the work surface, with the adhesive side facing upwards. Do not stick it to the pattern. The pattern should be completely covered by the vinyl yet visible through it. Tape in place, taking care not to position tape within the pattern outline.

NOTE Use, if possible, clear 8 mil sandblast resist material for the strength of its adhesive and the thickness of the vinyl. It is available at most stained glass shops. As an alternative, use clear contact paper which can be purchased at most department and hardware stores. However, its adhesive is not as good

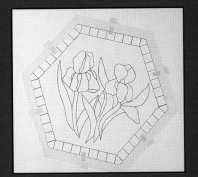

Trim the pattern to fit inside the mold with 1/2 in (1.3 cm) clearance between sides and pattern.

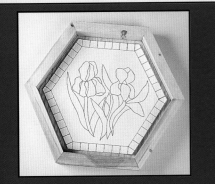

The vinyl should be 1/2 in (1.3 cm) larger than the pattern.

and the glass pieces may not stick to it as well as to the resist.

Drawing an accurate pattern outline for the 16 in (40.6 cm) hexagonal garden stone Several glass mosaic projects have been designed for garden stones using a 16 in (40.6 cm) hexagonal mold/form. A 16 in (40.6 cm) plastic mold is available commercially at many stained glass supply shops or you can make your own wood form as described on p77. You can draw an accurate pattern outline for these projects by following the steps listed below.

Materials
1 piece of grid paper 24 in x 24 in (60.9 cm x 60.9 cm)

Tools
Cork-backed straightedge
Pencil
Permanent waterproof fine-tipped marker
Eraser

1 With pencil and straightedge, draw 3 parallel horizontal lines, from one end of the grid paper to the other. These lines must be exactly 8 in (20.3 cm) apart and the middle line must be positioned in the center of the paper. *See* diagram at right.

2 Mark the center point on each line. Connect these points by drawing a vertical line, perpendicular to the three horizontal lines.

3 On the top and bottom horizontal lines, place a mark 4⅝ in (11.7 cm) on either side of the vertical line.

4 On the middle horizontal line, place a mark 9¼ in (23.5 cm) on either side of the vertical line.

5 On the right-hand side of the vertical line, draw straight lines connecting the marks on the bottom and top lines with the mark on the middle line. Repeat on the left side.

6 Verify the accuracy of the

hexagonal outline. Each of the six sides should be 9¼ in (23.5 cm) long and the measurement between opposite sides will be 16 in (40.6 cm). The distance from opposite corners will be 18½ in (46.9 cm).

7 Trace the outline with the marker and straightedge. Erase pencil lines outside the hexagon. If required, the lines inside the hexagon can act as guides when drawing your pattern.

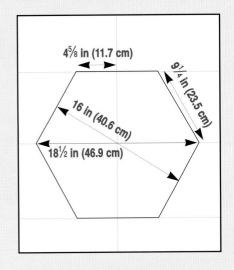

Preparing the glass pieces
1 Using the first copy of the pattern and the marker, trace (pp13–4) each pattern piece onto the glass to be cut. Do not trace each of the numerous tesserae pieces of the same size and shape required for some projects. Each pattern requiring these pieces will specify the size and number of pieces to cut.

2 Cut (pp14–22) each piece of glass required, making sure to cut inside the marker line. Use the cork-backed straightedge to assist in scoring straight lines and tesserae pieces (pp19, 21–2).

3 Smooth or grind any glass edges that are jagged or do not fit the pattern (pp22–3). Remember, the glass mosaic construction method does not insist on the precision needed to make a stained glass

window. The pieces should fit inside the pattern lines, leaving at least $\frac{1}{16}$ to $\frac{1}{8}$ in (0.15 to 0.3 cm) space between each piece to allow cement around the individual pieces for a smoother finish and a better bond to the garden stone.

4 Clean each piece thoroughly to ensure adhesion to the clear adhesive-backed vinyl. Remove all traces of cutter oil, marker, grinding residue, etc. with soap and water. Rinse thoroughly with clean water.

Placing the glass pieces   You are now ready to place the cut glass pieces onto the clear adhesive-backed vinyl. Remember, the pattern copy under the vinyl is the reverse of the pattern you used to cut the glass pieces. Turn each glass piece over and place face down onto the vinyl in the correct position. Press the pieces firmly onto the resist.

Transferring the glass pieces to the form/mold   Once all the glass pieces have been pressed onto the clear adhesive-backed vinyl, the form/mold must be prepared before the glass is placed inside.

1 Coat the interior sides of the form with a thin layer of petroleum jelly. All sides, edges, and corners must be lubricated to make releasing the garden stone easier.

2 Apply petroleum jelly on approximately 1 in (2.5 cm) only around the perimeter of the bottom of the form, where the sides meet the bottom. If the entire bottom piece of the form is coated with petroleum jelly, it will act as a large suction cup, making it more difficult for the stone to release from the form.

3 Using a utility knife, cut away the excess vinyl on the outside edges of the pattern, getting as close to the edges of the glass as possible without dislodging any pieces.

4 Carefully lift the vinyl with the adhered glass pieces and place in the center of the form with the glass side facing upwards. The vinyl acts as a barrier between the form and the glass (for easy removal from the form) and to help prevent movement of the individual pieces while pouring the cement.

5 If the form/mold is flexible in any way, place a piece of plywood underneath the mold. Plywood or metal forms will not require this but most plastic molds will flex or bend if moved or picked up before the wet cement mixture has set.

Reinforcing   Before mixing and pouring the cement into the form/mold, prepare the reinforcement wire. Galvanized hardware cloth (wire mesh) is best. Cut the hardware cloth to fit within the form/mold, making it approximately 1 in (2.5 cm) smaller all around the perimeter to prevent the wire from poking through the concrete on the sides of the garden stones.

Pouring the cement
A fine grade of ready-mixed cement or mortar mix will provide a smooth surface for any glass mosaic garden stone. Coarser grades of sand will leave a pitted surface. Be sure to follow the manufacturer's instructions.
NOTE When cement mixes are combined with water, a caustic, calcium hydroxide solution is formed. Avoid contact with skin areas, eyes, and clothing. Always wear safety glasses or goggles, work apron, rubber or latex gloves, and a respirator or dust mask when mixing and pouring cement. Whenever possible mix cement outdoors. This will prevent the active ingredients and dust in the cement mixture from entering your work area and/or home.

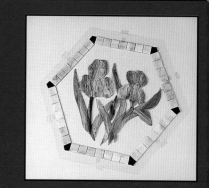

Leave a space between pieces to allow cement around each piece fc a better bond to the garden stone.

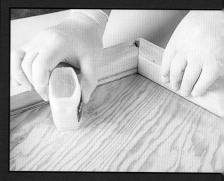

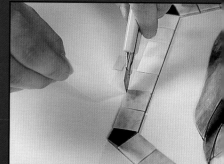

Coat the inside of the mold to make the release easier. Trim vinyl as close to pattern edge as possible without dislodging the glass. Carefully set the vinyl with glass pieces into center of mold/form.

A fistful of cement squeezed in your hand should maintain its shape when you open your fingers.

Pour a layer of cement into the mold/form, tapping down to release air bubbles. Add the wire mesh. Continue to fill the form and smooth out top with a trowel.

Wash with water immediately, any skin areas or clothing that come in contact with wet cement mixtures.

1 Mix the dry contents of the mortar mix first, so bonding agents are evenly distributed. The entire bag (an average size is 55 lbs or 25 kg) should be well mixed to ensure a quality pour even if you use only a portion of the mix.

2 Once the dry ingredients have been mixed thoroughly, empty the contents of the bag into a watertight container. Add the amount of water required (approximately 1 gal or 4 liters) and mix until the ingredients are well blended. The mixture should be moist but not runny or crumbly (a fistful of the cement squeezed in your hand should maintain its shape when you open your fingers). Allow the cement to stand for 5 minutes, then re-mix thoroughly.

3 Carefully place a handful of the cement mixture into the form. Gently smooth cement around the edges and over the glass, being careful not to dislodge any pieces from the vinyl. With your hand, gently pat the mixture to release trapped air bubbles and assist cement in working its way into the spaces between the glass pieces. Add enough cement to fill the form halfway and continue patting. Tapping softly on the work surface with a hammer or mallet will produce the same results.

4 Place the precut reinforcement wire onto the cement and pour enough of the cement mixture on top to fill the form. Again, gently pat for several minutes to release air bubbles. The entire depth of the garden stone will be approximately 1½ to 2 in (3.8 cm to 5 cm), depending on the form/mold used.

5 After patting for several minutes you will notice water on the surface.

This is normal. Level the top of the garden stone with a trowel or straight piece of wood.

NOTE You can make your own cement mixture as an alternative to the ready-mixed commercial varieties. Add 3 parts of fine grade sand to 1 part of portland cement. Mix the dry ingredients thoroughly. Add water and mix until the desired consistency is achieved. Trial and error will result in finding the right mix.

Adding tints to the cement mixture

Tints in powder and liquid form can be added to the concrete mix before pouring it into the form/mold. At which stage of the cement pouring process the tint is added depends on the type of tint. Read the manufacturer's instructions carefully. Choose a color tint that will enhance the glass pieces of the garden stone.

Curing

1 Set the poured garden stone form/mold on a level surface that has been covered with plastic sheeting or newspaper to protect the work surface from leakage. The form should be kept out of direct sunlight and covered with plastic sheeting to prevent the cement mixture from drying too quickly. Leave undisturbed for a minimum of 3 to 5 days. Do not allow to freeze. *See* photo p74.

2 Once the cement has set, mist with water once a day to make sure it is not drying too quickly.

Releasing the garden stone from the form/mold

Once the cement mixture has set and become concrete, it is time to unveil the glass mosaic garden stone.

1 After the cement has set and cured, the garden stone can be released from the form/mold. On a work surface that has been covered with

newspaper, turn the form over and lay it face down.

2 The stone is ready to be removed from its form.

WOOD FORMS Unscrew the bottom piece from the attached side pieces. Unscrew two side pieces on opposite ends of the form so that they can be pulled apart, splitting the form into two halves. Pull the two halves away from the garden stone, releasing it completely from the form. To reuse the form, simply screw the side and bottom pieces back together.

PLASTIC MOLDS Invert the mold and lay it face down on the work surface. With one hand, tap on the bottom of the mold while slightly raising one side of the mold off the table with the other hand. Rotate the mold while continuing to tap until the stone has released from the mold. Care should be taken to not use too much force.

3 Peel the clear adhesive-backed vinyl from the top of the garden stone. With a water dampened sponge or cloth, wipe away the thin film of cement on the glass surface.

4 Excess cement can be removed with a soft bristled brush or by carefully scraping it away with a razor blade, paint scraper, or utility knife. Dental picks and toothbrushes can be used to clear away bits of cement caught in grooves in the glass.

5 Small pits caused by trapped air bubbles or gaps between glass pieces can be filled in. Mix a small batch of ready-mix mortar and smooth over the surface with a damp sponge or cloth. Add tint if it was used in the original pour. Allow the mortar to dry to a thin haze for approximately 10 minutes and then wipe away excess with a damp sponge.

6 If you continue to have problems removing unwanted cement from the surface of the glass pieces, try using

muriatic acid. Because of its hazardous properties, handle it with care. Read the label carefully and follow all safety precautions. Muriatic acid can be found at your local hardware store and should be used only as a last resort.

7 With a dry cloth, buff the surface of your new glass mosaic garden stone.

8 It will take about 30 days for the concrete to fully cure so take a little care when handling the garden stone. It should not be placed outside before it has cured completely if there is the possibility of freezing. Refrain from walking on garden stones until fully cured.

Installing the finished glass mosaic garden stone

It is time to place the finished mosaic stone in its rightful place— your garden! Once you have chosen its special location, set it into the ground or nestle it amongst some foliage.

To set it in the ground

1 Place the stone on

Cure the stone for a minimum of 3 to . days. Mist once a day. Do not freeze.

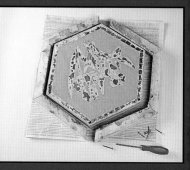

Unscrew the bottom piece and pull the form into two pieces.

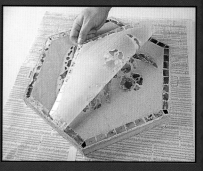

Peel back the vinyl to reveal the garden stone mosaic pattern.

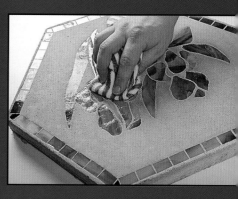

Carefully remove excess cement from glass surface, regrout pitted areas, and polish with a soft cloth.

the ground in its chosen position. With a small garden spade or shovel, break the ground around the perimeter of the stone. Remove the stone and dig a hole the depth of the stone plus ½ in (1.3 cm).

2 Fill the bottom ½ in (1.3 cm) of the hole with sand and tamp it down, making sure it is level. This will act as drainage for any moisture that may occur.

3 Place the garden stone in the hole. It should be at ground level to prevent people from tripping over the stone and lawnmower blades from damaging or scratching the glass.

Caring for and maintaining your garden stone

Once the garden stone is installed, it requires little maintenance. It can be left in the garden all year round regardless of the temperature. Here are some general care requirements.

1 Stones that are part of a water garden or exposed to much moisture, should be stored in a dry place during periods of freezing and thawing.

2 Stains and mildew can be removed from stones by scrubbing the surface with a diluted solution of chlorine bleach and water.

Help! Why didn't my garden stone turn out?

Before starting a garden stone, review the instructions given. A less-than-perfect outcome can occur if all the appropriate steps and techniques are not carried out. Here are a few tips and guidelines that will help you avoid trouble.

1 Glass pieces immersed in the cement
To prevent
• Before being placed on the clear adhesive-backed vinyl, glass pieces must be clean and free of any cutter oil or glass residue from grinding.

When transferring into the mold, avoid getting petroleum jelly (used to coat the inside of the mold) on the glass or the vinyl.

• Firmly press the smoothest side of the glass pieces onto the sticky side of the vinyl. The wet cement mixture may seep between the glass and the vinyl if textured glass pieces are positioned with the textured surface adhered to the vinyl.

• For the strongest adhesion qualities, use 8 mil clear sandblast resist. Vinyl contact paper (sometimes referred to as shelf paper) with a strong tack can also be used. To maintain the adhesive integrity, refrain from placing anything but the appropriate glass pieces onto the vinyl.

• Care must be taken when filling the mold/form with the wet cement mixture and when patting the cement to release trapped air bubbles. Patting the cement with too much force may dislodge glass pieces from the vinyl.

To correct
• If a glass piece is partially covered by cement, scrape away the excess cement with a razor blade, paint scraper, or utility knife. Dental picks are a useful tool for digging cement out of grooves in the glass.

• A glass piece that is completely immersed can often be uncovered. Check the surface of the garden stone for a slight halo (outline) of the piece. With a fresh razor blade, carefully scrape away the cement until the glass piece is revealed. If required, mix and apply a small amount of cement to the stone surface to smooth out any gouges or unevenness caused while excavating the glass piece.

• If the whereabouts of a glass piece is not known, it is advisable to leave

Top: Glass pieces immersed in the cement.
Bottom: Surface of garden stone is pitted.

it undisturbed. Once the stone has been situated in the garden or walkway, the concealed piece will probably not be missed.

2 Surface of garden stone is pitted
To prevent
• A space (also known as an interstice), at least 1/16 to 1/8 in (0.15 cm to 0.3 cm) wide, must be present between each glass piece. This will allow the wet cement mixture to work its way around the perimeter of each piece and fill in the air spaces between the pieces.

• Use a fine grade of ready-made mortar mix. If making your own cement mixture, use a fine grade of sand. Cement mixtures containing coarse sand particles may not be able to fit into the interstices between the glass pieces.

• After filling the mold/form with the wet cement mixture, release trapped air bubbles and pockets by gently patting the cement for several minutes. Lightly tapping the work table surface with a mallet or hammer will also work.

To correct

• Fill in pits and level the surface of the garden stone by regrouting. Prepare a small amount of the wet cement mixture and spread over the top and sides of the stone, forcing the mixture into every crevice. With a water-dampened sponge, remove excess cement mixture and smooth out the garden stone's surface. Allow the cement to dry. A thin haze or film will be present on the glass pieces and can be wiped off with a dry cloth as soon as the cement has completely dried.

NOTE If a tint was added to the original cement mixture, add a proportionate amount of the color to the grout mixture.

3 Glass pieces have become dislodged from the garden stone surface

To prevent

• Thoroughly mix all cement ingredients to distribute them evenly throughout the cement mixture. This will ensure a proper bond. Store unused dry ingredients indoors, in a moisture-free environment.

• When transferring the sheet of clear adhesive-backed vinyl (with the glass pieces firmly attached) into the mold/form, be sure to position the vinyl so that there is at least ¼ in (0.6 cm) space between the edges of the mold and the glass pieces. The glass pieces must be completely surrounded by the concrete to hold them in place. Pieces that are too close to the outside edge of the garden stone may become detached or easily pried away from the stone's surface.

• Do not move a poured garden stone until the cement has cured and become concrete. Be sure to place plastic molds on a sturdy plywood sheet to transport from one area to another. Plastic molds are not rigid and will flex under the weight of the cement. This will cause everything to shift inside the mold and may result in glass pieces lifting from the vinyl and becoming encased in the wet cement.

To correct

• A glass piece that has come away from the garden stone's surface can be reattached. With a utility knife, smooth out the inside edges and bottom of the hole left by the glass piece. Remove any debris in the crevice. Spread a layer of water-resistant tile adhesive on the side edges and bottom of the glass piece and press into the opening. Allow to dry for a minimum of 24 hours. Grout around the glass piece and the opening with a small amount of wet cement mixture. Buff with a dry cloth once the cement has set completely.

4 Edges of garden stone are crumbling and breaking away

To prevent

• It is very important to mix the ingredients well to ensure proper adhesion and strength in the concrete. Follow the manufacturer's instructions carefully.

• Do not remove the garden stone from the form/mold prematurely. Depending on the aridity of the climate, the concrete must have at least 3 to 5 days to cure and harden. While curing, cover the mold/form with a plastic sheet and mist with water once a day. This will prevent the cement from drying too quickly. Keep out of direct sunlight.

To correct

• Try to strengthen the garden stone and improve its appearance by regrouting. Mix a portion of the wet cement mixture and apply it to the damaged areas. With your hands

Top: Glass pieces have become dislodged from the garden stone surface. Bottom: Edges of garden stone are crumbling and breaking away.

(wear protective gloves) or a trowel, smooth the cement onto the stone and shape it to the correct dimensions. Cover with a plastic sheet and let dry slowly, misting occasionally. Once hardened, clean the excess concrete off the surface of any affected glass pieces.

Making your own garden stone forms

There are a variety of commercial forms and molds available to hobbyists. A number of household items can also be used such as baking tins, springform cake pans, plastic food storage containers, etc. However, if you want a certain shape and size form/mold but it is not readily available, making one is not difficult.

Wood forms

Wood forms are easy to make and

can be used many times. In fact, wood is preferable when making square, rectangular, or hexagonal forms. You will need a few wood-working tools and the knowledge to use them safely. When using power tools, read the manufacturer's directions and follow all safety guidelines and precautions. Always wear an apron and safety glasses.

Materials
1 copy of pattern
¾ in (1.9 cm) plywood
2 x 2 in (5 cm x 5 cm) framing lumber
No.8 wood screws (2½ in or 6.4 cm in length)
Sandpaper

Tools
Apron
Safety glasses
Marking pen or pencil
Drawing or carpenter's square
Cork-backed straightedge
Wood saw (hand or power)
Power drill with drill bits suitable for woodworking
Screwdriver
NOTE Use ¾ inch (1.9 cm) plywood (because of its strength and durability) for the form base. It can withstand the weight of the cement and will not warp. A garden stone should be approximately 1½ in to 2 in (3.8 cm to 5 cm) in depth. Use 2 in x 2 in (5 cm x 5 cm) framing lumber to make the sides of the form (framing lumber measures approximately ½ in or 1.3 cm less than the designated size). The sides provide support and contain the wet cement mixture within the form until it sets and becomes concrete.

Making hexagonal forms
Hexagonal garden stone patterns in this book have been designed to fit the standard 16 in (40.6 cm) plastic hexagonal mold available at stained

glass stores. If you prefer a wood form it is simple to make.

BASE PIECE
1 Using the project pattern as your guide, trace the outline of the hexagon onto the center of a 24 in x 24 in (60.9 cm x 60.9 cm) sheet of ¾ in (1.9 cm) plywood.
2 Draw a 1½ in (3.8 cm) perimeter around the traced outline, to accommodate the addition of the side pieces.
3 With the wood saw, cut the larger hexagon base piece out of the plywood sheet.

SIDE PIECES
4 Cut six lengths of 2 in x 2 in (5 cm x 5 cm) framing lumber.
5 Using the protractor as a guide, mark a 30° angle at either end of each piece. The outside edge of each side piece needs to measure 11 in (27.9 cm), with the inside edge measuring 9¼ in (23.5 cm), when cut.
6 Cut the ends of each piece at the 30° angle marked.

ALIGNING AND ATTACHING THE SIDE PIECES TO THE BASE
7 Using the original pattern outline as a guide, align two adjacent side pieces and butt the angled ends together. Fasten the two side pieces together with a wood screw.
8 Repeat the procedure with each side piece, creating a six-sided frame.

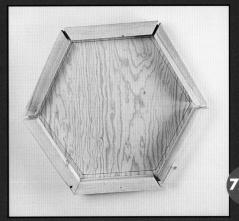

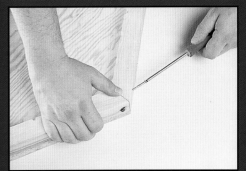

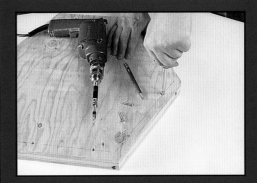

Butt side pieces together and fasten with wood screws. Turn form over and fasten base to side pieces with wood screws.

9 Place the plywood base piece on top of the frame. Fasten with 2 wood screws per side.

10 If required, smooth any rough surfaces or edges on the wooden form with sandpaper.

NOTE To make wood screws easier to twist in, mark and predrill holes in the side pieces and base. Using wood screws instead of nails to construct a wood form allows the user to take the form apart if the finished garden stone cannot be easily removed. Damage to the garden stone is prevented and the form can easily be screwed back together and used again.

Making square and rectangular forms

BASE PIECE

1 Measure the width and height of the garden stone pattern. Add 3 in (7.6 cm) to each measurement to allow room for the attachment of the form side pieces. For example, a 16 in x 16 in (40.6 cm x 40.6 cm) square garden stone requires a plywood base 19 in x 19 in (48.3 cm x 48.3 cm).

2 With a marking pen and straightedge, mark the dimensions required for the base onto the plywood sheet.

3 Using a wood saw, cut the base piece away from the main sheet of plywood.

SIDE PIECES

4 Measure each side of the pattern outline. Add 1½ in (3.8 cm) to each side measurement, mark, and cut the 2 in x 2 in (5 cm x 5 cm) framing lumber. For a square garden stone pattern measuring 16 in (40.6 cm) along each side, cut four lengths that measure 17½ inches (44.5 cm).

ALIGNING AND ATTACHING THE SIDE PIECES TO THE BASE

5 Using the pattern as your guide, lay a side piece along the corresponding edge of the garden stone outline. One end of the piece should start at a corner (where two sides meet at a right angle) with the other end extending past the pattern outline, approximately 1½ in (3.8 cm).

6 Proceed to align the next side piece. Butt one end of the second piece against the overlap of the first side piece. As with the preceding side, the opposite end of the piece will extend past the pattern outline by approximately 1½ in (3.8 cm). Fasten the two pieces together with a wood screw.

7 Repeat step 6 to align and fasten each of the two remaining side pieces, creating a four-sided frame. Use a drawing or carpenter's square to verify that each corner is square.

8 Place the plywood base on top of the frame and fasten, using 2 wood screws per side.

9 If required, smooth any rough surfaces or edges on the wood form with sandpaper.

Styrofoam and plywood forms

Circular and irregular shape forms, such as the ones used to create the Interlocking Footprints garden stones project (p93), can be made with styrofoam and plywood. Use high density insulation styrofoam, used by the construction industry, available at hardware stores. Although these forms are not as durable as wood, plastic, or metal forms/molds, they can be used several times if handled with care.

Materials
1 copy of pattern
Carbon paper
Masking tape
Styrofoam sheet (approximately 2 in or 5 cm thick)
¾ in (1.9 cm) plywood
Water-resistant adhesive

Tools
Apron
Safety glasses
Marking pen or pencil
Utility knife
Wood saw (hand or power)
Power drill

1 Place carbon paper face down over the center of the styrofoam sheet. Position the pattern copy over the carbon paper and fasten in place with masking tape.

2 Trace the outline of the pattern onto the styrofoam sheet. The styrofoam must be large enough to allow at least 2 in (5 cm) of space between the pattern outline and the edge of the sheet. Remove the carbon and pattern copy.

3 Pull the knife toward you along the traced outline in a steady and smooth motion. Do not use an up-and-down sawing motion. The knife must be held perpendicular to the work surface and cut all the way through the styrofoam.

4 Remove the cut styrofoam from the center of the sheet.

5 Cut a plywood base piece the same size as the styrofoam sheet.

6 Apply a water-resistant adhesive to the underside of the styrofoam sheet and press firmly to the plywood base. Allow to dry, following the manufacturer's instructions.

7 Verify that the project pattern fits within the form.

8 Drill several holes through the middle of the base piece. If the garden stone is not easy to remove from the form, you will be able to push against the stone surface through the holes with a piece of wood doweling. This will aid in releasing the finished stone.

NOTE Apply a thin layer of petroleum jelly to the sides and inside edges of all forms and molds, regardless of the materials used in their construction.

Garden Stones tabletop and chairs

Patios and decks can be enhanced by turning a stained glass mosaic garden stone into a durable outdoor tabletop and chairs. Place the stone on top of a metal base or support that can be found at your local stained glass shop. These bases fit a variety of shapes and sizes of garden stones. If you wish to make your own table supports, bend and weld steel rods into geometric or exotic shapes. Creating the base can be an interesting venture and you can choose a design and shape to fit your project.

You can also have the base custom made at your local metal fabrication shop.

To design a stained glass mosaic garden stone tabletop or chair you can convert one of the following patterns to the appropriate size.

Iris Duet

MOLD REQUIRED   16 in (40.6 cm) hexagonal
TOTAL NUMBER OF PIECES   82
WET MORTAR-MIX CEMENT REQUIRED   21 cups
GLASS REQUIRED   Letters refer to the type of glass used on pattern pieces (p81).
The quantity of glass is the exact amount needed for the pattern. To allow for matching textures and grain you may have to purchase more glass.

A   6 in x 7 in (15.2 cm x 17.8 cm) blue and green ring mottle (cut into 1 in x 1 in or 2.5 cm x 2.5 cm tesserae pieces—42 pieces)
B   3 in x 6 in (7.6 cm x 15.2 cm) yellow and white wispy
C   6 in x 8 in (15.2 cm x 20.3 cm) iridized purple and white wispy
D   9 in x 8 in (22.8 cm x 20.3 cm) iridized green and white wispy
E   6 in x 3 in (15.2 cm x 7.6 cm) green and white wispy

1 Construct this project by following the instructions given for Construction Techniques (pp70–4).
2 Prepare the pattern by referring to *Drawing an accurate pattern outline for the 16 in (40.6 cm) hexagonal garden stone* (p71).
3 Use a purchased 16 in (40.6 cm) hexagonal form/mold or make your own form. See *Making your own garden stone form* (pp77–8).

Flower Power

MOLD REQUIRED   16 in (40.6 cm) hexagonal
TOTAL NUMBER OF PIECES   79
WET MORTAR-MIX CEMENT REQUIRED   21 cups
GLASS REQUIRED   Letters refer to the type of glass used on pattern pieces (p81).
The quantity of glass is the exact amount needed for the pattern. To allow for matching textures and grain you may have to purchase more glass.

A   2 in x 5½ in (5 cm x 13.9 cm) cranberry pink and white wispy
B   6 in x 8 in (15.2 cm x 20.3 cm) pink and white wispy
C   6 in x 6 in (15.2 cm x 15.2 cm) light blue and white wispy
D   4 in x 5 in (10.1 cm x 12.7 cm) purple and white wispy
E   4 in x 5 in (10.1 cm x 12.7 cm) yellow and white opaque
F   6 in x 8 in (15.2 cm x 20.3 cm) yellow and white wispy
G   6 in x 8 in (15.2 cm x 20.3 cm) white and clear wispy
H   4 in x 5 in (10.1 cm x 12.7 cm) dark blue and white wispy
I   7 in x 6 in (17.7 cm x 15.2 cm) green and white wispy
AA   amber glass nugget (medium)
BB   light blue glass nugget (large)
CC   yellow glass nugget (large)
DD   white glass nugget (medium)
EE   dark blue glass nugget (medium)
FF   dark purple glass nugget (large)
GG   amber glass nugget (large)
HH   yellow glass nugget (medium)

1 Construct this project by following the instructions given for Construction Techniques (pp70–4).
2 Prepare the pattern by referring to *Drawing an accurate pattern outline for the 16 in (40.6 cm) hexagonal garden stone* (p71).
3 Use a purchased 16 in (40.6 cm) hexagonal form/mold or make your own form. See *Making your own garden stone form* (pp77–8). NOTE Glass nuggets make interesting accents on any garden stone. When positioning them on the clear adhesive-backed vinyl, be sure to press the flat (bottom) side of the nugget onto the vinyl. Nuggets may become immersed in the cement if placed with the rounded side face down. Cut glass pieces can be substituted for glass nuggets.

HELPFUL HINT There are two sizes of flower petals used for this pattern. To make tracing and cutting the glass pieces easier, make a template (p14) of the small and large petals. Use the templates to trace the required petal shapes onto the glass. Following this step will save time and glass.

See photograph, p68.

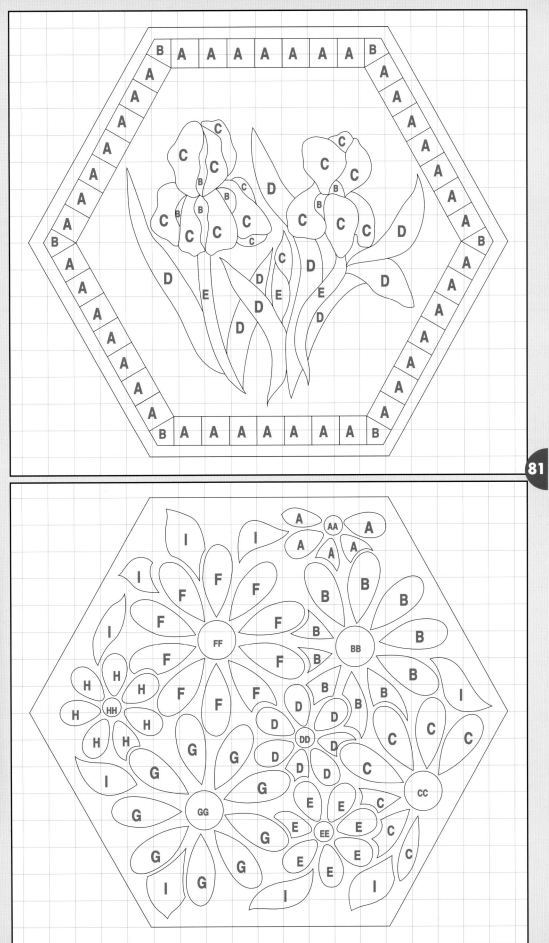

Mr. Sunshine

MOLD REQUIRED   16 in (40.6 cm) hexagonal

TOTAL NUMBER OF PIECES   98 plus background tesserae

WET MORTAR-MIX CEMENT REQUIRED   21 cups

GLASS REQUIRED   Letters refer to the type of glass used on pattern pieces (p83).

The quantity of glass is the exact amount needed for the pattern. To allow for matching textures and grain you may have to purchase more glass.

A   12 in x 12 in (30.5 cm x 30.5 cm) orange opaque (cut 18—1¼ in x 1¼ in or 3.1 cm x 3.1 cm tesserae and use balance to cut face and outer sun ray pieces)

B   7 in x 12 in (17.8 cm x 30.5 cm) orange and white wispy (cut 18—1 in x 1 in or 2.5 cm x 2.5 cm tesserae and use balance to cut outer sun ray pieces)

C   2 in x 3½ in (5 cm x 8.9 cm) red and white wispy

D   1 in x 1 in (2.5 cm x 2.5 cm) iridescent black

E   4 in x 4 in (10.1 cm x 10.1 cm) yellow and white wispy (cut 60—½ in x ½ in or 1.3 cm x 1.3 cm tesserae pieces)

F   2 iridescent green glass nuggets (medium)

1 Construct this project by following the instructions given for Construction Techniques (pp70–4).

2 Prepare the pattern by referring to *Drawing an accurate pattern outline for the 16 in (40.6 cm) hexagonal garden stone* (p71).

3 Use a purchased 16 in (40.6 cm) hexagonal form/mold or make your own form. See *Making your own garden stone form* (pp77–8).

NOTE Glass nuggets make interesting accents on any garden stone. When positioning them on the clear adhesive-backed vinyl, be sure to press the flat (bottom) side of the nugget onto the vinyl. Nuggets may become immersed in the cement if placed with the rounded side face down. Cut glass pieces can be substituted for glass nuggets.

Special instructions

Positioning the tesserae

The tesserae for this project are applied using the *opus vermiculatum* method, p27.

1 Use the outlines of the pattern as a guide and place the sun ray tesserae (A and B) firmly onto the clear adhesive-backed vinyl.

2 The tesserae (E), required to fill in the background of the sun face are the last pieces of glass to be laid on the vinyl. Begin applying a row of tesserae around the perimeter of the sun face, following the contours of the pieces that have already been applied. Using the glass cutter or the mosaic nippers, trim a tessera to fit into spaces that are not large enough to accommodate a whole piece. Once you have completed an entire row around the face, start a new row inside the one just completed. Fill in the entire background of the sun face using this method.

NOTE A space of at least ¹⁄₁₆ in (0.15 cm) must be left between and around each glass piece.

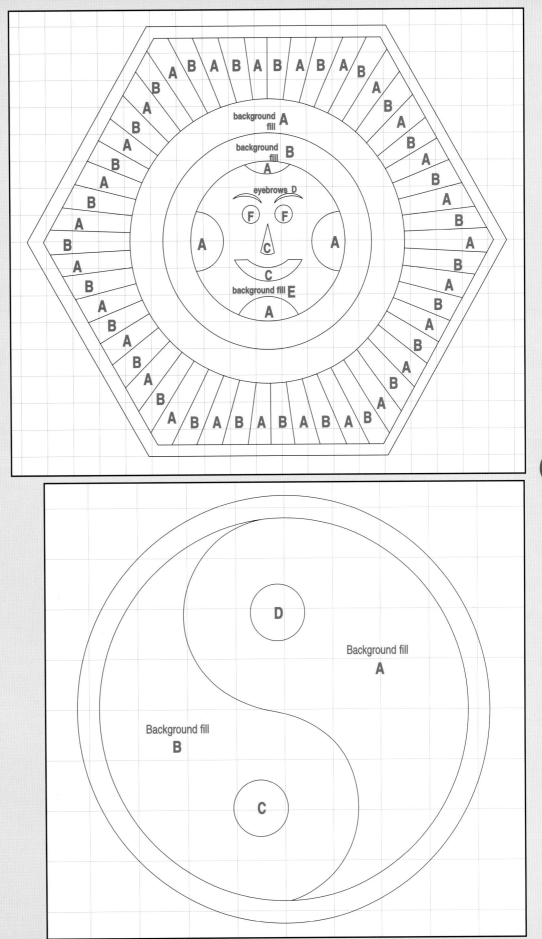

Ying & Yang

MOLD REQUIRED   8½ in (21.6 cm) circular form
TOTAL NUMBER OF PIECES   172 (approximate)
WET MORTAR-MIX CEMENT REQUIRED   9 cups
GLASS REQUIRED   Letters refer to the type of glass used on pattern pieces (p83).
The quantity of glass is the exact amount needed for the pattern. To allow for matching textures and grain you may have to purchase more glass.

A   4 in x 6 in (10.1 cm x 15.2 cm) black (cut into ½ in x ½ in or 1.3 cm x 1.3 cm tesserae pieces)
B   4 in x 6 in (10.1 cm x 15.2 cm) white (cut into ½ in x ½ in or 1.3 cm x 1.3 cm tesserae pieces)
C   black glass nugget (large)
D   white glass nugget (large)

1 Construct this project by following the instructions given for Construction Techniques (pp70–4).
2 Use an 8½ in (21.6 cm) circular form/mold such as a standard 8½ in (21.6 cm) springform baking tin or make your own form. See *Making your own garden stone form— Styrofoam and plywood forms* (p78).

Special instructions
Positioning the tesserae
The tesserae for this project are applied using the *opus vermiculatum* method, p27. Tesserae are positioned to follow exactly the outline of the pattern and around the glass nuggets. The stark contrast between the glass pieces and the simple lines of the pattern are clearly accentuated using this method.
1 Apply the glass nuggets to the clear adhesive-backed vinyl. Press the flat (bottom) side of the nugget onto the vinyl. Nuggets may become immersed in the cement if placed with the rounded side face down. Cut glass pieces can be substituted for the glass nuggets, if you prefer.
2 Tesserae (A and B) required to fill in the rest of the garden stone can now be laid on the vinyl. Begin applying a perimeter row of tesserae (A) within the pattern outline. Using the glass cutter or the mosaic nippers, trim a tessera to fit into spaces that are not large enough to accommodate a whole piece. Once you have completed an entire row around the perimeter, start a new row inside the one just completed. Using this method, fill in the entire background of this section.
3 Repeat this procedure for the remainder of the tesserae (B).
NOTE A space of at least 1/16 in (0.15 cm) must be left between and around each glass piece. Refer to the photograph of the finished project to see how this application technique is achieved.

Eternity

MOLD REQUIRED 9½ in (24.1 cm) circular form

TOTAL NUMBER OF PIECES 200 (approximate)

WET MORTAR-MIX CEMENT REQUIRED 11 cups

GLASS REQUIRED Letters refer to the type of glass used on pattern pieces (p87).
The quantity of glass is the exact amount needed for the pattern. To allow for matching textures and grain you may have to purchase more glass.

A 3½ in x 5 in (8.9 cm x 12.7 cm) iridescent blue cathedral
B 5 in x 10 in (12.7 cm x 25.4 cm) iridescent clear texture (cut into ½ in x ½ in or 1.3 cm x 1.3 cm tesserae pieces) NOTE One side of this glass selection must be smooth.

1 Construct this project by following the instructions given for Construction Techniques (pp70–4).
2 Use a 9½ in (24.1 cm) circular form/mold such as a standard 9½ in (24.1 cm) springform baking tin or make your own form. See *Making your own garden stone form— Styrofoam and plywood forms* (p78).

Special instructions Clear textured glass and a colored cathedral glass have been used for this project. Normally, clear glass is not recommended. However, the iridescent finish on these glass selections has a beautiful reflective quality and makes the underlying concrete unnoticeable.

Placement of the glass pieces
1 Using the pattern as your guide, place each of the iridescent blue cathedral pieces (A) iridescent side face down onto the clear adhesive-backed vinyl.

Positioning the tesserae
Tesserae (B) are cut from iridescent clear textured glass. Be sure to lay the smooth side of the tesserae face down onto the vinyl. If the textured side of the tesserae is placed against the vinyl, the wet cement mixture may work its way into cracks and crevices in the glass causing the tesserae to lift from the vinyl and become immersed in the concrete.
1 Apply the border tesserae (B) to the vinyl.
2 The infill tesserae (B) have been placed onto the vinyl in undulating rows. Use the photo as a guide when positioning the tesserae. Using the glass cutter or the mosaic nippers, trim a tessera to fit into spaces that are not large enough to accommodate a whole piece. Fill in the entire background using this method.
NOTE Be sure to leave a space of at least ¹⁄₁₆ in (0.15 cm) between and around each tessera piece.

Grapes

A   31 purple and iridescent purple glass nuggets (medium)

B   5½ in x 4½ in (13.9 cm x 11.4 cm) green and white ring mottle

C   3 in x 6 in (7.6 cm x 15.2 cm) amber and brown (cut random-size tesserae no larger than ½ in or 1.3 cm in width)

1 Construct this project by following the instructions given for Construction Techniques (pp70–4).
2 Use a 10 in (25.4 cm) circular form/mold such as a standard 10 in (25.4 cm) springform baking tin or make your own form. See *Making your own garden stone form— Styrofoam and plywood forms* (p78).

Special instructions

Placement of the glass pieces
1 Using the pattern as your guide, place each leaf piece (B) face down onto the clear adhesive-backed vinyl.
2 A mixture of purple and iridescent purple glass nuggets has been used to represent grapes. Be sure to press the flat (bottom) side of the glass nugget onto the vinyl. If you place the rounded side face down the nuggets may become immersed in the cement. Cut glass pieces can be substituted for the glass nuggets.
NOTE Glass nuggets vary greatly in size. Use the garden stone pattern as a guide when positioning the glass nuggets on the vinyl and add or leave out nuggets as required to fit the pattern. For a different look,

substitute the suggested purple nuggets with a mixture of green and iridescent green ones.

Positioning the tesserae
1 When cutting the vine tesserae pieces, refer to *Cutting random-size tesserae* (pp21–2). Tesserae pieces for this project should not be wider than

½ in (1.3 cm).
2 Use the vine outlines on the garden stone pattern as a guide when placing the random-size tesserae onto the vinyl.
NOTE Be sure to leave a space of at least 1/16 in (0.15 cm) between and around each tessera piece.

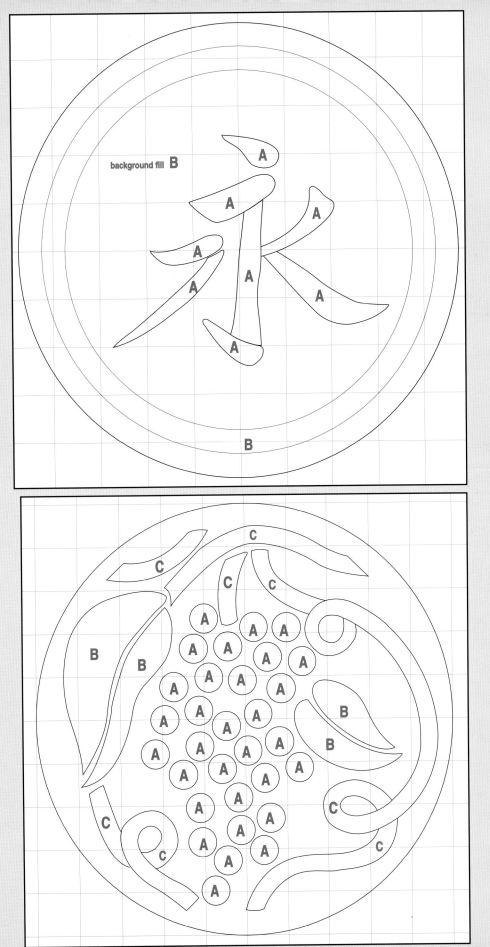

background fill **B**

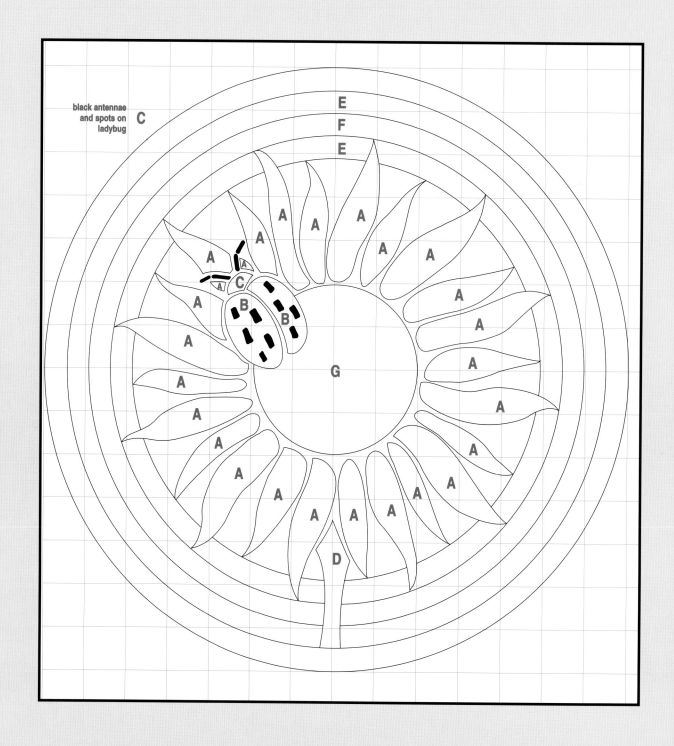

black antennae
and spots on
ladybug

A   7 in x 11 in (17.8 cm x 27.9 cm) yellow and white wispy

B   2 in x 2 in (5 cm x 5 cm) iridescent red and white wispy (cut into random-size tesserae approximately ¼ in x ¼ in or 0.6 cm x 0.6 cm)

C   2 in x 2 in (5 cm x 5 cm) black

D   3 in x 1 in (7.6 cm x 2.5 cm) dark green and white wispy

E   6 in x 7 in (15.2 cm x 17.8 cm) deep sky blue opaque (cut into random-size tesserae, maximum width ½ in or 1.3 cm)

F   4 in x 5 in (10.1 cm x 12.7 cm) iridescent white (cut into random-size tesserae, maximum width ½ in or 1.3 cm)

G   4 in x 4 in (10.1 cm x 10.1 cm) amber and brown opaque (cut into random-size tesserae approximately ½ in x ½ in or 1.3 cm x 1.3 cm)

1 Construct this project by following the instructions given for Construction Techniques (pp70–4).

2 Use a 14 in (35.5 cm) circular form/mold such as a commercial mold available at stained glass supply shops or make your own form. See *Making your own garden stone form —Styrofoam and plywood forms* (p78).

Special instructions   Glass pieces must be laid on the clear adhesive-backed vinyl in a particular order. Refer to the accompanying photograph of the finished stone for individual piece placement.

Placement of the glass pieces

1 Place cut glass pieces (C) for the ladybug antennae, head, and spots onto the vinyl. Arrange the remaining tesserae (B) pieces on the vinyl for the ladybug body using the pattern outline as a guide.

2 Place the sunflower petals (A) and the stalk (D) onto the vinyl in the correct positions.

3 Lay the random-size tesserae pieces (G) in circular rows for the center of the sunflower. Apply a row of tesserae around the perimeter of the sunflower center, beginning and ending on either side of the ladybug body. Using the glass cutter or mosaic nippers, trim a tessera to fit into any space that is not large enough to accommodate a whole piece. Continue by laying a new row inside the one just completed. Fill in the entire center in this manner.

4 Fill in the border rows with the random-size tesserae (E and F) required.

NOTE Be sure to leave a space of at least 1/16 in (0.15 cm) between and around each tessera piece.

Snake & Lizard

MOLD REQUIRED   14 in (35.5 cm) circular form

TOTAL NUMBER OF PIECES   177 (approximate)

WET MORTAR-MIX CEMENT REQUIRED   20 cups

GLASS REQUIRED   Letters refer to the type of glass used on pattern pieces (p91).
The quantity of glass is the exact amount needed for the pattern. To allow for matching textures and grain you may have to purchase more glass.

A   28 red glass nuggets (small)

B   4 dark blue nuggets (medium)

C   ⅞ in x 5¾ in (2.2 cm x 24.6 cm) white wispy (cut 10—1 in x 1 in x 1 in or 2.5 cm x 2.5 cm x 2.5 cm triangles)

D   ⅞ in x 5¾ in (2.2 cm x 24.6 cm) dark blue and white wispy (cut 10—1 in x 1 in x 1 in or 2.5 cm x 2.5 cm x 2.5 cm triangles)

E   4 in x 4 in (10.1 cm x 10.1 cm) orange and white wispy

F   4 in x 1½ in (10.1 cm x 3.8 cm) red and white wispy

G   4 in x 4 in (10.1 cm x 10.1 cm) iridescent dark green and white wispy

H   4 in x 2½ in (10.1 cm x 6.3 cm) iridescent white

J   4 in x 5 in (10.1 cm x 12.7 cm) black

NOTE   The letter I has not been used on this listing.

1 Construct this project by following the instructions given for Construction Techniques (pp70–4).

2 Use a 14 in (35.5 cm) circular form/mold such as a commercial mold available at stained glass supply shops or make your own form. See *Making your own garden stone form —Styrofoam and plywood forms* (p78).

NOTE   Glass nuggets make interesting accents on any garden stone. Be sure to press the flat (bottom) side of a glass nugget onto the adhesive-backed vinyl. If you place the rounded side of the nugget face down on the vinyl, it may become immersed in the cement. Cut glass pieces can be substituted for glass nuggets.

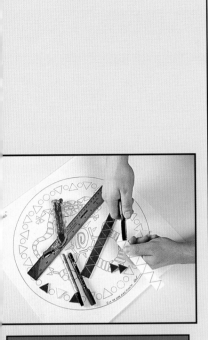

HELPFUL HINTS
A. To avoid waste of glass, position the 1 in (2.5 cm) triangular pattern pieces (C and D) on the ⅞ in x 5¾ in (2.2 cm x 24.6 cm) strips of glass, as shown.
B. After cutting the glass pieces for the sun rays (E), cut remainder into random-size tesserae that will fit within the outline of the sun center.

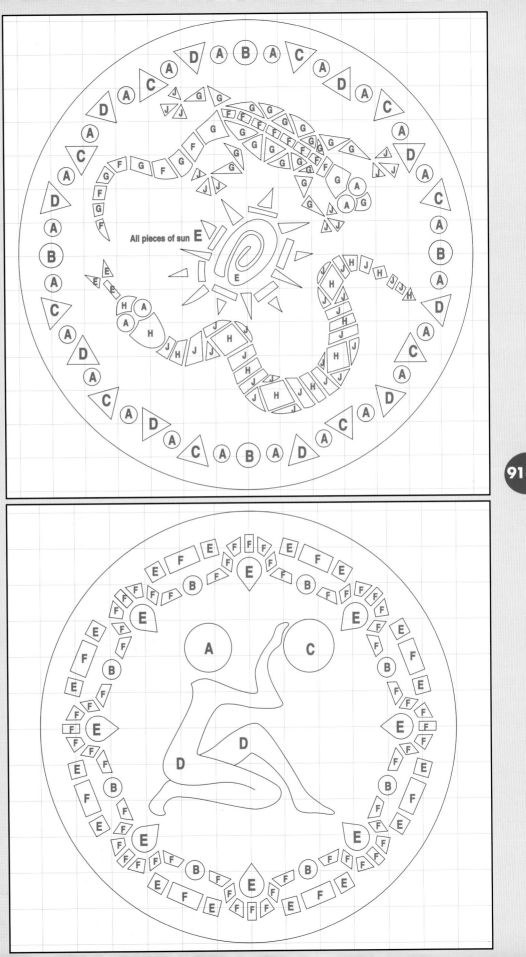

Sun-sational

MOLD REQUIRED   12 in (30.5 cm) circular form

TOTAL NUMBER OF PIECES   250 (approximate)

WET MORTAR-MIX CEMENT REQUIRED   14 cups

GLASS REQUIRED   Letters refer to the type of glass used on pattern pieces (p91).
The quantity of glass is the exact amount needed for the pattern. To allow for matching textures and grain you may have to purchase more glass.

A 1 red glass nugget (large)

B 8 red glass nuggets (small)

C 2 in x 2 in (5 cm x 5 cm) iridescent amber cathedral

D 5 in x 5 in (12.7 cm x 12.7 cm) iridescent amber and white opaque (cut into ¼ in x ¼ in or 0.6 cm x 0.6 cm tesserae pieces)

E 4 in x 4 in (10.1 cm x 10.1 cm) peach and white wispy

F 5 in x 4 in (12.7 cm x 10.1 cm) green, tan, and white opaque streaky

1 Construct this project by following the instructions given for Construction Techniques (pp70–4).
2 Use a 12 in (30.5 cm) circular form/mold such as a 12 in (30.4 cm) plastic food storage container or make your own form. See *Making your own garden stone form— Styrofoam and plywood forms* (p78).
NOTE Glass nuggets make interesting accents on any garden stone. Be sure to press the flat (bottom) side of a glass nugget onto the adhesive-backed vinyl. If you place the rounded side of the nugget face down, it may become immersed in the cement. Cut glass pieces can be substituted for the glass nuggets.

HELPFUL HINTS

A. Make a template to cut the smaller border pieces (F) (p14).
1 Lay a 4 in x 4 in (10.1 cm x 10.1 cm) piece of card stock on the work surface and place a carbon sheet face down overtop. Place the border section of the project pattern on top and fasten in place with push pins or tape. Trace the outline of the pattern pieces, pressing firmly so that the image is transferred through to the card stock.
2 With a utility knife, cut along the inside of the traced lines, making sure not to cut past the lines.
3 Unfasten the card stock from the work surface and remove the cutouts from the main piece.
4 Place the card stock on the glass and trace the outline of the cutout pieces with a permanent marker.
5 To cut the glass, score on the outside of the traced line. This will ensure that the piece is cut to the correct size.
B. When smaller tesserae are required for a project, it is easier to cut a larger size tessera into a few pieces of the smaller size. Use the glass mosaic cutters (nippers) or a glass cutter to divide a tessera in half and then into smaller shapes and sizes.
C. Accentuate the curves of the figure by placing the tesserae (D) along the pattern outlines of the body. Refer to the photograph to see how this effect is accomplished.

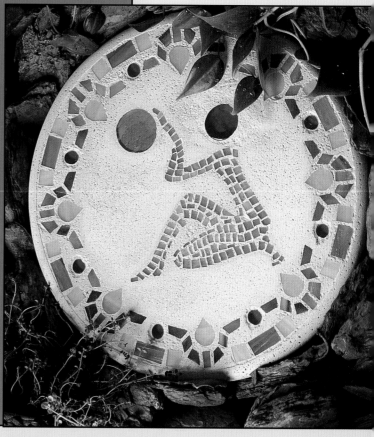

Interlocking Footprints

MOLD REQUIRED   interlocking form
TOTAL NUMBER OF PIECES   15 plus background pieces
WET MORTAR-MIX CEMENT REQUIRED   14 cups
GLASS REQUIRED   Letters refer to the type of glass used on pattern pieces (p94).
The quantity of glass is the exact amount needed for the pattern. To allow for matching textures and grain you may have to purchase more glass.

Material requirements, measurements, and instructions are for one stone.

A   9 clear glass nuggets (medium)
B   6 in x 3½ in (15.2 cm x 8.9 cm) iridescent clear texture
C   miscellaneous glass pieces

Make enough "footprints" garden stones for an interesting border around a special tree or flower bed. If you move the pattern around, the footprints can create an interesting walkway around your garden.

1 Construct this project by following the instructions given for Construction Techniques (pp70–4).
2 Make your own interlocking garden stone form. See *Making your own garden stone form—Styrofoam and plywood forms* (p78).

NOTE Glass nuggets make interesting accents on any garden stone. Be sure to press the flat (bottom) side of a glass nugget onto the adhesive-backed vinyl. If you place the rounded side of the nugget face down, it may become immersed in the cement. Cut glass pieces can be substituted for the glass nuggets.

Special instructions

1 Use leftover glass pieces from other projects for the background of these garden stones. Be sure to place glass pieces at least ½ in (1.3 cm) from the outside edge of the form.
2 If a garden stone is too large to fit with another one, make the interlocking part of the stone smaller by filing it when it is first released from the mold and the cement is still soft or malleable.

NOTE Cover the work surface with newsprint and wear a respirator or dust mask. If possible, work outdoors to prevent the spread of concrete dust in your workshop or home.

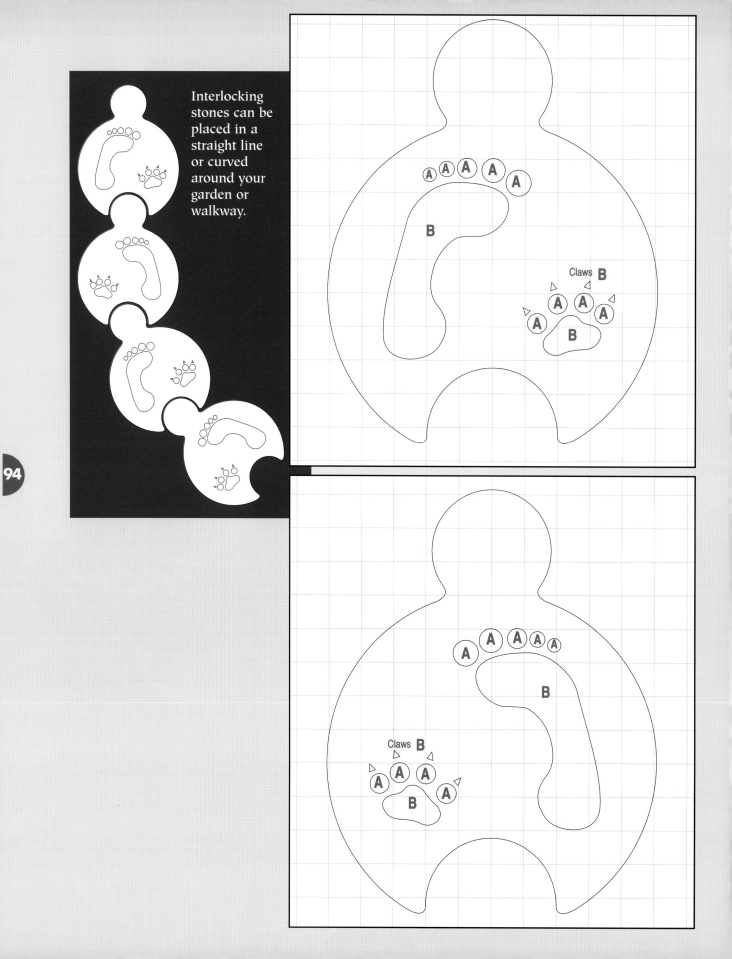

Interlocking stones can be placed in a straight line or curved around your garden or walkway.

About the authors

George W. Shannon and Pat Torlen began working with stained glass as a hobby but it quickly evolved into a way of life with the opening of their shop, On The Edge Glass Studio in Winnipeg, Canada. The studio offers a wide range of classes and workshops for hobbyists of all skill levels. As well as teach, Pat and George design and fabricate commissioned works for commercial and residential clientele utilizing traditional and contemporary stained glass techniques, sandblasting, and kiln work. Through the years both artists have participated in workshops given by internationally renowned glass artists. George has attended a workshop at Pilchuck Glass School in Stanwood, Washington. Their first book, *Stained Glass: Projects & Patterns*, was published in 1995 by Sterling/Tamos.

Greta Torlen shares her sister's enthusiasm for glass and has played an important role in furthering glass art in Winnipeg. She teaches classes in stained glass mosaic and has been instrumental in adapting traditional mosaic applications for the materials and tools used by stained glass hobbyists. She is also interested in glass painting and learned about traditional methods in classes conducted by Richard Mallard.

Index

adhesive, 6, 12, 27, 28, 30, 31, 32, 36, 39, 44, 63, 64, 76
adhesive-backed vinyl, 6, 29, 30, 31, 32, 44, 70, 71, 72, 73, 74, 75, 76, 81, 82-5, 86, 89, 93
Ankara, 5
apron, 12, 14, 23, 32, 77
Art Nouveau, 5

background fill, 27, 30
backsplash, 62
backsplash mounting, 63, 64
Barcelona, 5
base/support structures, 7, 26, 27, 30, 31, 32, 33, 34, 36, 48, 51, 53, 55, 58, 63, 64, 66
basic techniques, 13-23
birdbath, 43
breaking glass on a score line, 14, 15, 18, 19
breaking pliers, 8, 13, 18, 19
brushes, 10, 28, 74
buffing, 28, 74
"buttering," 27, 28, 64
Byzantine, 5

carbon paper, 7, 13, 14, 26, 78, 92
carborundum stone, 10, 11, 20, 22, 23, 26
cement, 6, 11, 12 72, 73, 74, 75, 76, 77, 85
cement pouring in mold, 72, 73
ceramic tiles, 6, 27, 41, 42
Chagall, Marc, 5
chairs (outdoor), 79
circular garden stone form construction, 78, 84, 85, 86, 89, 90, 92
classical system, 5
cleaning finished mosaics, 27, 28, 32, 36, 42, 67
Cock-a-Doodle-Dude pattern, 51
Cock-a-Doodle-Dude trivet, 50
combination pliers, 8, 18, 19, 20, 21
concrete, 11, 12, 73, 76, 77, 85
Constantinople, 5
construction techniques (garden stones), 70
construction techniques (projects), 26
contact paper, 6, 29, 71, 75
containers, 10, 28, 39, 42, 73
cork pads, 33, 34
curing, 45, 67, 73, 74, 76
cutting random-size tesserae, 21, 22
cutting uniform tesserae, 21, 22

direct method construction technique (projects), 26-8, 29, 39, 42, 44, 45, 48, 51, 53, 55, 58, 63, 66
direction change glass effect, 55
Distraction wall hanging & trivet, 57
Distraction wall hanging & trivet pattern, 59
drawing equipment, 7, 8
dust mask (respirator), 11, 12, 23, 72, 93

Early Christian, 5
Eternity garden stone, 85
Eternity garden stone pattern, 87

Fish Faerie backsplash, 62
Fish Faerie backsplash pattern, 64
float glass, 14

Flower Power garden stone, 80
Flower Power garden stone pattern, 81
Flowers planter box, 35, 36
Flowers planter box pattern, 37
form/mold, 10, 70, 71, 72, 73, 74, 75, 76, 82
form/mold (stone removal), 73, 74
found objects, 5
framing materials, 33, 34, 77, 78

galvanized hardware cloth (wire mesh), 7, 72
garden stones, 69
garden stone construction errors, 75, 76
garden stone form hexagon pattern, 71
garden stone installation, 74, 75
garden stone maintenance, 75
garden stone plastic mold, 71, 76, 77
garden stone release from form, 73, 76, 78
garden stone styrofoam forms, 77, 78
Garden Stone tabletop, 79, 80
garden stone wood form circle construction, 78
garden stone wood form hexagon construction, 77, 78
garden stone wood form square & rectangle construction, 78
Gaudi, Antoni, 5
glass bandsaw, 63
glass breaking, 14, 15, 18, 19, 20, 21, 22
glass cutters, 8, 14, 15, 19, 20, 21
glass cutting, 14, 15, 16, 17, 19, 20, 21, 42
glass cutting practice patterns, 14, 16, 17
glass grinder, 10, 20, 22, 23
glass mirror, 34, 66
glass mosaic cutters, 8, 21, 23, 36, 37, 39
glass mosaic techniques, 27
glass nuggets, 6, 45, 81, 82, 84, 86, 90, 92, 93
glass pieces preparation, 26, 29, 44, 71
glass selection, 13, 70
glass tapping, 18, 19
Grapes garden stone, 86
Grapes garden stone pattern, 87
grout, 6, 12, 27, 28, 36, 39, 42, 44, 45, 63, 67
grozing pliers, 8, 20, 21
gloves, 12, 23, 28, 72, 73, 76

Hellenistic Greeks, 5
Herbs planter box, 35
Herbs planter box pattern, 37

indirect (reverse) method construction technique (projects), 29-32, 36, 44, 45
Interlocking Footprints garden stone, 93
Interlocking Footprints garden stone pattern, 94
In-the-Eye-of-the-Beholder wall mirror, 65
In-the-Eye-of-the-Beholder wall mirror pattern, 67
intestices, 6, 75
iridescent cathedral glass, 6, 13, 70, 85
Iris Duet garden stone, 80
Iris Duet garden stone pattern, 81
Italian Renaissance, 5

jars, 10, 27
jigsaw, 63

keying, 26, 30
Klimt, Gustav, 5

light box, 11, 14
light table, 11, 29, 70
Lily Pond birdbath, 43
Lily Pond birdbath pattern, 46
limestone, 5
Lizards cactus pot pattern, 40
Lotus & Dragonfly wall hanging, 47
Lotus & Dragonfly wall hanging pattern, 49

marble, 5
Mr. Sunshine garden stone, 82
Mr. Sunshine garden stone pattern, 83
mitering, 33
modern method, 5
molds/forms, 10, 70-6
mortar cement, 6, 44, 45, 72, 73, 74, 75
mosaic construction, 5
mosaic tabletop, 60
mosaic technique, 5
mounting mirrors, 34, 67
mounting wall hangings, 34
muriatic acid, 74

newspaper, 10, 11, 14, 73, 74
nippers, 8, 21, 22, 36, 37, 39, 45, 82, 89
notched trowel, 10, 30

Old Tiles terra-cotta pot, 41
opaque glass, 6, 13, 14, 29, 55
opus tesselatum method, 27, 36, 51, 55, 64
opus vermiculatum method, 27, 64, 82, 84

paint scraper, 10, 28, 32, 45, 74, 75
palette knife, 27, 36
pattern copying, 13, 14, 26, 29, 61
pattern (16 in hexagonal garden stone), 71
pattern from upholstery, 61
pattern preparation, 26, 29, 44, 70
pattern transfer onto glass, 13, 14
pattern transfer onto support structure, 26
pebble technique, 5
petroleum jelly, 6, 72, 75, 78
placing glass onto vinyl, 30, 36, 44
placing glass pieces, 70, 72, 85, 89
planter boxes, 35, 36
plywood, 7, 32, 33, 34, 61, 63, 64, 77, 78
polishing cloths, 10
polishing mosaic, 28
portland cement, 6, 73
power tools, 32, 77

random method, 27, 36, 42, 45, 53, 58
reinforcement wire, 7, 75, 76
Relativity wall hanging & trivet, 54
Relativity wall hanging & trivet pattern, 56
removing garden stone from mold, 73, 74
repairing pitted stone, 74, 75, 76
Romans, 5
"running," 18, 19, 20, 21
running pliers, 10, 18, 20, 21, 22

safety clothing, 12, 23
safety glasses, 11,12, 14, 21, 22, 23, 32, 77
safety practices, 12, 23, 32, 72, 73, 93
sand, 6, 72, 73, 75
sandblast resist, 6, 29, 71, 75
scoring glass, 14, 18, 19, 20, 21

sectioning mosaic piece, 30, 31, 32, 36
semi-precious stones, 5
silicon, 10, 66
silicone sealant, 39, 42, 64, 66
smalto(i), 5
smoothing sharp glass edges, 10, 22, 27, 71
Snakes cactus pot pattern, 40
Snakes & Lizards cactus pots, 38
Snake & Lizard garden stone, 90
Snake & Lizard garden stone pattern, 91
St. Peter's Basilica, 5
sponges, 10
springform baking pan, 10, 76, 84, 85, 86
stained glass, 5, 6, 13, 25
stained glass mosaic construction, 6
Stained Glass Mosaic tabletop, 60
stained glass tesserae, 21
styrofoam forms (garden stones), 78
Sunflower & Ladybug garden stone, 88
Sunflower & Ladybug garden stone pattern, 88
Sunflower wall hanging, 33, 52
Sunflower wall hanging pattern, 53
Sun-sational garden stone, 92
Sun-sational garden stone pattern, 91

tabletop (indoor), 60, 61, (outdoor), 79
tapping, 18, 19, 20
template, 14, 21, 29, 70, 81, 92
terra-cotta pots, 28, 38, 39, 41, 42
terra-cotta pot grid, 42
tessera(e), 5, 21, 22, 26, 27, 28, 30, 36, 39, 44, 45, 52
tiles, 5
tints, 6, 73, 74, 76
tracing, 13, 14, 26, 29
traditional method, 5
transferring glass pieces to mold, 72, 76
translucent glass, 6, 13, 85
trivets, 32, 33, 50, 54, 57
turning mosaic sections, 31, 32
tweezers, 10, 28, 30
trowel, 10, 30, 44, 73, 76

utility knife, 10, 26, 28, 30, 32, 45, 63, 72, 74

Vatican, 5

wall hangings, 32, 33, 34, 47, 52, 54, 57
wall mirror base, 33
water lilies, 44, 45
water lily pattern, 46
waterproof fine-tipped marker, 7, 13, 14, 21, 23
window tracing, 29
wire cutters, 10
wire mesh, 7, 72, 73
wood forms (garden stones), 74, 76, 77, 78
wood support structures (projects), 32, 33, 34, 36, 48, 51, 53, 55, 58, 63, 64, 66
wood trim, 7, 33, 34, 61
woodworking tools, 11, 32, 33, 77, 78
work area, 11, 12

Ying & Yang garden stone, 84
Ying & Yang garden stone pattern, 83